Paul Mallard has provided wonderful support and encouragement for anyone going through difficulties and struggles in life. One comment he makes sums it up: 'It is better to trust God in the darkness than to try to find consolation in a fake theology that offers help, but ends in confusion and despair.' His biblical illustrations of how God understands suffering are beautifully described, and he gives the best explanation of the suffering, death and resurrection of Christ that I have ever read. His honesty will bring comfort and hope to anyone who has questions about life's trials.

Fiona Castle, speaker and author, widow of Roy Castle

With immediacy and tenderness, Paul Mallard probes the acute problem of our pain and suffering. Interlacing his chapters with an honest appraisal of the human condition, he allows us a glimpse into some of his own and his wife's deep experiences of trial and suffering over many years. Yet throughout he points continually to the compassion and mercy of God, closing on a note of triumph which lifts our eyes beyond our own circumstances to the coming glory when all wrongs will be righted forever.

Faith Cook, writer and speaker

Walking with a family in their personal suffering can be a sad experience, this one is exhilarating. Deeply embedded in this moving story of Paul and Edrie's battle with chronic disability is the strong steel of a theology of suffering that rests on the caring providence of a loving and wise God. In a way that few can, the author responds biblically and creatively to why God brings intense sorrow into the life of the Christian. It will encourage the sufferer, inspire the doubter and challenge the unbeliever.

Brian H. Edwards, author, lecturer and teacher

With this book, Paul Mallard makes a fresh contribution to the literature on suffering for three main reasons: firstly, he writes with the authority born from his personal experience: 'You can talk about pain with some credibility when people see you have walked this road,' he

D0266744

says. Secondly, the work is full of biblical wisdom, combining a 'good dose of biblical realism' (in his own words) with the inspiring promises and hope that are ours through Jesus and become 'an anchor for the soul, firm and secure' (Hebrews 6:19). Thirdly, it is a book written with a warm pastoral heart. Full of practical insights and help for everyday life, *Invest Your Suffering* offers the reader a real gold mine for their own times of trouble. I am sure its reading will not disappoint anyone who, like myself, has walked through this valley before.

Dr Pablo Martinez, psychiatrist and author of A Thorn in the Flesh: Finding Strength and Hope Amid Suffering

This book is an inspiring love story, conceived in eternity but forged through pain and suffering. From beginning to end it is a moving expression of Paul's love for his wife Edrie, as they both struggle with the reality of her long-term debilitating illness, and of their love for God, as they determine to trust his good and sovereign purposes, whatever the circumstances.

Scarily honest, this book is insightful, inspiring and, above all, informed by Scripture. It is a must-read for all of us who struggle with the pain of a broken world and wish to support our fellow-strugglers.

Highly recommended!

Richard Underwood, Pastoral Director of FIEC

INVEST
YOUR
SUFFERING

PAUL MALLARD

INVEST YOUR SUFFERING

UNEXPECTED INTIMACY WITH A LOVING GOD

INTER-VARSITY PRESS
Norton Street, Nottingham NG7 3HR England
Email: ivp@ivpbooks.com
Website: www.ivpbooks.com

British Library Cataloguing in Publication Data
A catalogue record for this book is available from the British Library.

ISBN: 978–1–78359–006–3
ePub: 978–1–78359–029–2
Mobi: 978–1–78359–030–8

Set in Dante 11.5/14pt
Typeset in Great Britain by CRB Associates, Potterhanworth, Lincolnshire
Printed in Great Britain by Ashford Colour Press Ltd, Gosport, Hampshire

*Inter-Varsity Press publishes Christian books that are true to the Bible and that
communicate the gospel, develop discipleship and strengthen the church for its mission
in the world.*

*Inter-Varsity Press is closely linked with the Universities and Colleges Christian
Fellowship, a student movement connecting Christian Unions in universities and colleges
throughout Great Britain, and a member movement of the International Fellowship of
Evangelical Students. Website: www.uccf.org.uk*

This book is dedicated to Edrie,
my girl now and forever

Contents

Foreword   11

1. The power and prevalence of pain   13
2. Clearing the decks of false ideas   23
3. A word from another world   39
4. Living in a broken world   51
5. Knowing the One who knows us perfectly   65
6. Perfect way, perfect purposes   77
7. Developing the family likeness   91
8. Reasons to be cheerful   105
9. Living with uncertainty   119
10. Don't waste your sorrows   133
11. The love that will not let us go   147
12. Living in hope   163

Notes   179

Foreword

It was less than a decade ago that I first met Edrie and Paul. Yet I already felt that I had known them a long time. Their experience of learning to cope with long-term, 'no-known-cure' disability so deeply mirrored that of Brenda my wife, an MS sufferer for nearly forty years, and myself. I only wish this book had been available to us back then, as we entered the dark tunnel of suffering and wondered if light might burst through in that tunnel and not only at its end. Now their story and wisdom are available to us all.

A wise man once wrote, 'God only had one Son without sin; he has no sons (or daughters!) without suffering.' So may I unreservedly encourage you to read this great little book and pass it on, for it will help you understand some of the reasons for that wise man's observation. Allow me to expand a little on why I am enthusiastically recommending this book.

First, the book deals with the great and recurring problem of suffering and a God of love. In my experience, for many people this is *the* reason for their professed indifference or antagonism to the gospel. *Invest Your Suffering* gently confronts many of the objections raised against Christian answers to why there is evil in the world. Be warned! Sceptics and agnostics may need to guard their 'faith' very carefully as a result!

Next, it deals with the great themes of the Bible, as it wrestles with the problem of pain in God's world. Paul Mallard allows Scripture to scatter its pearls of wisdom and explode its star-bursts of hope, bringing illumination, challenge and comfort to the weary, the hopeless and the confused.

Paul also writes with great pastoral insight, sensitivity and warmth, and not a little humour. Here's a couple who really have 'been there, done that and got the T-shirt' in the school of suffering. Yet, bravely and together, without airbrushing out the dark days and the rough paths, they have held firmly to the faith, and discovered that the Lord has firmly and faithfully held on to them.

One of my favourite Greek words is *Tharsei*. It means: 'Be encouraged!' That is precisely what I have discovered in reading and being helped by this book. I believe you will too.

Dr Steve Brady
Principal
Moorlands College
Christchurch, Dorset

1. The power and prevalence of pain

It is a warm June morning as I hurriedly comb Keziah's hair. Keziah is my bright and beautiful five-year-old daughter. We have to leave for school in a few minutes. Keziah sits on the stairs and I sit a little further up. To my shame, I have to admit I had never combed her hair before and I am not making a very good job of it. I attack the tangles like an explorer carving his way through the Amazon rainforest.

Suddenly, she bursts into tears. 'Daddy, you are hurting me!' she cries.

For me, this is the last straw. I begin to sob.

Her tears are quickly forgotten as she looks up into my face, puts her hand in mine and asks, 'What's the matter, Daddy?'

I probably shouldn't have said it so bluntly, but I couldn't help myself.

'I just want Mummy back. I want her to be well.'

I grew up a working-class family in Birmingham in the 1960s. I had always been taught that real blokes don't cry. And yet there I was, sitting on the stairs sobbing like a baby in front of my confused and slightly alarmed daughter. Never before had I experienced such pain. It felt as if I was losing the only girl I had ever loved.

True love sometimes runs smoothly

Edrie and I weren't exactly childhood sweethearts. We had gone to the same junior school and first got to know each other at church. Her dad was one of the leaders, and I was a local kid who started attending after a summer holiday outreach. We became friends in our early teens and started courting just before I left Birmingham to go to university. We already knew each other pretty well and soon fell in love. She was vivacious and gorgeous and the most life-affirming person I had ever met. I was awkward and shy and exceedingly gauche. We were perfect for each other!

Everything about Edrie was unique – including her name. She was called after her grandmother. Most people think the name is Welsh. Actually, it is taken from 'Edrei', an obscure village mentioned in some of the early books of the Bible. It is sometimes described as the 'habitation of giants', which is slightly ironic since my wife stands five feet two inches tall!

Our courtship lasted five years. During that time, our love deepened and matured. So did the conviction that God was calling me into some form of full-time Christian ministry. When I proposed to Edrie, I took her to a windswept hill overlooking the beautiful city of Birmingham, and, as if on cue, the snow began to fall. I got down on my knees and asked her the question she knew was coming.

'I want you to marry me, but I have to tell you that you will always be the second person in my life. God has to come first, and, what is more, I think he is calling me into full-time service.'

Not the most romantic proposal ever – but at least it was honest!

'Of course the answer is yes,' she replied, 'and I want God to be first as well.'

We got married six months later. Edrie had been my first girlfriend, and I could not imagine being with anyone else.

Early years

The early years of married life were great. We had moved down to Wiltshire, so that I could teach religious education in a large comprehensive school. After five years, I left teaching to become the pastor of the church where we worshipped. The people were kind, and the work grew steadily. We both felt we were in exactly the right place.

After ten years of marriage, we had had three children, and the church was flourishing. Happiness is hard to define and even harder to hold on to, but I can honestly say we were truly and deeply happy.

Of course, there were dark and difficult times. There would be illness and deaths in the family, and we would experience no fewer than three miscarriages.

And our relationship was (and is) not perfect – in spite of what some people may tell you, no relationship ever is. We were two imperfect people in a very imperfect world, but God was so kind to us, and our love helped us through most things. Life was good, very good. We had the same sense of humour, and amid the pressures of church life and bringing up a growing family, we could always laugh together. We often commented on how blessed we felt. If I had believed in luck, I would probably have said that we were very lucky indeed.

All change

This particular trial began in such a low-key way. Edrie was pregnant with our fourth child and was having a really rough time. She suffered intense nausea and could manage nothing more than sips of cold water. After about three weeks, she seemed to feel better, but then began to complain about a sensation of 'fullness' in her ears. Soon after, she began to experience a loss of balance. During the Easter break, we attended a Christian conference, and she found it difficult to walk or even stand. She began to slur her speech, manifesting all the symptoms of someone who had been drinking too much alcohol – not what you expect at a large national meeting of Christians!

When we got home, we visited the GP, and he admitted her to hospital, to the Ear, Nose and Throat (ENT) Department. He told us it might just be a problem with the inner ear, and the specialists would soon sort her out. Everyone at church kept assuring me that, once the pregnancy was over, she would get better. They would smile sagely and shake their heads: 'Pregnancy does strange things to a woman's body.' I wanted to believe that, very much. But although I was concerned and anxious, at this stage I wasn't really frightened. Edrie had always been so vivacious and full of life. She would soon get better. It never crossed my mind that this illness might change our lives forever.

One day I turned up at the ENT Department, only to be told that my seven months pregnant wife had been transferred to Neurology. The title unnerved me. I had visited patients in Neurology before, and it always seemed to be bad news. What would it mean for us?

The answers, or non-answers, came very quickly. The consultant neurologist looked very serious when he told us that he wanted Edrie to have a lumbar puncture, followed quickly by an MRI scan. The lumbar puncture was very painful for her: how do you lie on your tummy when you're seven months pregnant? And the MRI was inconclusive. But all the time, my wonderfully brave wife kept her sense of humour. When I brought the kids to visit her, she would embrace them warmly and pull all three onto the bed. For the next hour, she would listen to the things that were troubling them, and comfort and reassure them. The visits always ended with family prayers. Whenever the kids prayed, it was always the same: 'Be with Mum when we are gone and bring her home soon. We love her very much, Lord, and we need her.' For their sake, as much as hers, I also tried to be brave, but it was slowly dawning on me that we were about to face our greatest crisis.

The grimmest moment was when the neurologist asked to speak to me alone. It was not normal to talk to the partner like this, but my wife was very fragile. The neurologist suspected that she had a serious condition, perhaps multiple sclerosis. This was not usually life-threatening, but the complications of the pregnancy and the intensity of the symptoms made it a dangerous situation. If she was going to recover, she would need my full support.

Fear is a terrible thing. It creeps into the mind and just won't go away. Suddenly, you notice things. It's terrible to admit, but you become aware of the struggles of disabled people for the first time. On one occasion around this very worrying time, sitting in the hospital coffee shop, I watched an elderly man hold a cup of tea tenderly to the lips of his wife, and I had to leave because I found it too painful. In this sort of situation, you realize that there is a whole world of pain out there and, very reluctantly, you are about to join the club.

The church was great, but I had to face the real possibility that my ministry might end if I became a full-time carer. How would we cope with that? What would we tell the children? Most of all, I just wanted my girl back. Back as she always had been since I had first come to know her in the youth group.

Those first visits to the hospital were twenty years ago. My ministry wouldn't end, but Edrie wouldn't get better either.

However, looking back and without being glib and simplistic, Edrie's illness and disability have given us a deeper insight into our relationship with God and aided us in our ministry to other people. You can talk about pain with some credibility when people see that you have walked their road.

And over these years, we have become convinced of two things.

1. Pain is intense and universal

Living in the middle of the book

Firstly, we have come to recognize the sheer magnitude and awful intensity of pain that exists in the world. We are surrounded by pain, and the only condition for suffering it is to live long enough to experience it. Suffering is one of the most consistent themes of the Bible. We live in a fallen, broken, bleeding world.

I once prepared a series of sermons on suffering, and the thing that struck me most was the fact that suffering is actually an underlying assumption throughout the Bible. If you pinch out the first two chapters of Genesis and the last two chapters of Revelation, suffering and pain is the common theme of everything in between. The human race comes from a pain-free zone where everything was 'very good' (Genesis 1:31). And God's people are heading for a pain-free zone where the curse of sin and all its consequences will be gone forever, and all things will be made new (Revelation 21:5). However, we're not there yet. We live in the middle of the book, a place marked by tears and death, mourning and pain (Revelation 21:4). Any Christian teaching that wants to take us away from that experience of pain and settle us into a kind of pre-heaven bliss is unbalanced and unhelpful, and, frankly, downright wrong.

Suffering is one of the most consistent themes of the Bible.

We need a good dose of biblical realism here. Human beings are born for trouble 'as surely as sparks fly upwards' (Job 5:7). (We will meet Job in the next chapter.) In one of the most sobering of all the psalms, Moses reflects on his experiences and affirms:

> Our days may come to seventy years,
> > or eighty, if our strength endures;
> yet the best of them are but trouble and sorrow,
> > for they quickly pass, and we fly away.
> (Psalm 90:10)

The Bible is an honest book. It knows all about frustration and bereavement, about childlessness and depression. It tells us that we suffer because we are human, and because we are Christians. Sometimes, we suffer because we are stupid and do sinful things. Sometimes, it's because we are faithful and do righteous things. Sometimes, there seems to be no cause at all, and suffering appears out of a cloudless sky.

Jesus knew all about pain. The Bible calls him 'a man of suffering, and familiar with pain' (Isaiah 53:3). He grew up under the shadow of the stigma of illegitimacy and was branded as insane, or as worse, by the leaders of his people. In real human flesh, he experienced hunger and thirst, weariness and frustration. His own family rejected him, and the crowds eventually turned against him. After being betrayed by a friend and deserted by all his companions, he experienced the injustice of an unfair trial and was tortured to death. Crucifixion had been invented by cruel and vicious people, and was just about the most painful and most shameful way to die. Worst of all, Christ tasted the ultimate loneliness of divine desertion as, on the cross, he who knew no sin became a sin offering for people like us (2 Corinthians 5:21). He experienced physical, psychological and spiritual pain more than anyone who has ever lived. As the hymn writer reflected on this, he wrote, 'Come, see if there ever was sorrow like his.'[1]

Any cheap and tawdry theology that teaches us that it is possible to escape pain in this world has to contend with the overwhelming testimony of the Bible. We live in the middle of the book.

Pastoral ministry for over thirty years has confirmed this first conviction. As I look out at the congregation on a Sunday morning, I know I am preaching to people who have suffered, who are suffering or who are about to suffer. For some, it is a struggle even to be at church in the first place.

For many people, it's the daily struggle with the effects of the chronic physical pain that colours their whole existence. Just getting through the day is a battle. Physical pain sweeps over them, while loved ones look on helplessly and close to despair. Physical pain becomes a filter through which all of life is tinted.

However, there are other forms of pain just as devastating in their effects. I think of the young couple who have been told that they can never have kids of their own. They leave the Mother's Day service with tears in their eyes. Or I consider the bereaved wife who has been so brave for so long, helping her husband battle terminal cancer. Now that the battle is over, she cannot see any reason to get out of bed in the mornings. 'I feel as if I have a lump of love and nowhere to put it,' she cries. Then there is the guy who has suffered severe depression for forty years and for whom the brightest day is grey and frightening.

At its heart, all emotional pain is a sense of loss. It began with Adam in Genesis. How he must have grieved over the loss of Eden! All of us live east of Eden. We lose our comforts, our earthly certainties and many things we once took for granted. Most of all, as life unfolds, we lose the people who have loved us and made our lives bearable.

Life is a tough journey. And Christians don't always tell the truth. When you ask them how they are doing, they will airily reply, 'Just great', but you know their lives are falling apart. Somehow, we think that if we admit we are struggling, we are letting the side down.

So my first conviction: pain is a universal fact.

2. You can choose to overcome pain

Triumphing in the middle of the book
However, I hold a second conviction just as firmly. It is that the world is full of pain, but also that it is full of people who triumph in the midst of their pain.

I have met so many Christians who have left me amazed at their courage and fortitude and their desire to bring glory to God through the agony they have suffered. I have seen it in my wonderfully brave and incredibly courageous wife. Edrie's story is not one of bitterness and defeat, but one of faith and triumph. I wouldn't be writing this book otherwise.

The 'middle of the book' is also full of people who triumphed in adversity, indeed in *multiple* adversities. Think of Job's patience, Ruth's persistence or Joseph's faithfulness. Think of Mary's love, Paul's faith or Stephen's hope. Most of all, think of the triumph of the 'Man of sorrows' who refused to turn from the pathway of pain that his Father had called him to walk along, and who transformed it into the way of salvation.

When pain becomes intense, we are driven to cast ourselves on God as our only source of comfort. Elisabeth Elliot was the widow of Jim Elliot, a missionary who died a martyr's death on a beach in South America. She expressed an experience common to all Christians:

> I am not a theologian or a scholar, but I am very aware that pain is necessary to all of us. In my own life, I think I can honestly say that out of the deepest pain has come the strongest conviction of the presence of God and of the love of God.[2]

How can this be so? Of course, as Elisabeth says, you do not need to be a theologian or a scholar to make such a statement, but its truth is based on firm theological convictions.

Over the last twenty years, as Edrie and I have walked with pain, weeping and laughing together, I have reflected on the

Bible's insights. Suffering has caused us to read God's Word in a new way. It is not that we discovered things that we did not know before; it is that we recognized the Bible was written to encourage people like us who were often experiencing the ravages of pain. So the Bible is about suffering, but it is also about overcoming it.

In our darkest times, these biblical convictions sustained Edrie and me. The strength we needed to persevere and prevail over pain flowed from our knowledge of the truth. And it was the truth that set us free – free to see pain as part of the tapestry of life that a sovereign and all-wise God was weaving for us.

How do we respond?

We often say glibly that pain is good for us. That is not entirely true, for it all depends on how we respond. Pain can make us better or it can make us bitter. We are not helpless victims: we can choose. The right response is not a leap into the dark, but a deliberate and reasoned decision to trust, based on clear theological convictions.

Bad things do, and will, happen to us, but it is how we respond that defines who we are. We can choose to be overwhelmed by despair and let it temper our outlook on life, or we can embrace the pain and cry from our bruised and battered hearts, 'Yet will I praise him.'

In the course of this book, we will engage with some of the great Bible passages that have brought light into Edrie's and my darkest moments.

Let's explore some of these biblical convictions. Let's make the choice to trust God and grow through our pain. Life in the middle of the book is certainly tough, but it is also full of people who overcome and persevere, and who bring glory to God through their suffering.

2. Clearing the decks of false ideas

Christians can be brilliant

Our ordeal began when I had taken Edrie to the hospital. Until that point, I had been pretty blasé about things – I had no idea that chronic illness was to be part of the plan for our lives. But after the transfer to Neurology and the warning from the doctor about the seriousness of Edrie's condition, the full magnitude of our circumstances began to dawn on me.

Now, Edrie and I have always been honest with each other. And she was aware that the neurologist had asked to see me. So, as soon as I returned to the ward, she said, 'Tell me what he said, and tell me everything.'

So I did.

At first she couldn't believe it. Then she began to cry. I drew the curtain round the bed and took her in my arms. She kept whispering in my ear, 'I'm so sorry; I'm so sorry.' I assured her that it was not her fault and that we would survive this together.

Needless to say, I went home feeling pretty sick and anxious that day.

When this sort of thing happens, you turn to the people who

love you most. Our family was fantastic. So too was the church. They rallied round and poured their love into our lives. I remember meeting with my fellow leaders. 'We are here for you and will give you whatever you require. Take as long as you need.' Some of our dearest friends rallied round with words of comfort and little treats for Edrie.

Then the news began to travel down the Christian bush telegraph. We received phone calls, letters and cards, from virtually every brand of Christian you can imagine. We received messages of support from charismatic Baptists and Reformed Anglicans. We had phone calls from traditional Pentecostals and progressive Brethren. We were encouraged by Presbyterians and Methodists and Congregationalists. People we had never met, some on the other side of the world, had heard about this pastor and the problems he and his pregnant wife were going through, and they were rising up in a wonderful wave of concern and comfort and compassion. I would turn up at the hospital with the cards and letters, and Edrie and I would be amazed at the kindness and generosity.

Christians can be brilliant.

That's when I hit him – well, almost!

But there was the usual batch of unhelpful and unbalanced fanatics. One man told me that Christians should never be sick. He said no Christian should ever have a headache or a cold or wear spectacles, or even go bald. It was all a matter of faith. God wants us to get better, but is prevented if we cannot build up our faith to some kind of 'miracle-generating level'. This man appeared well-meaning, but it was clear that there was going to be no meeting of minds. I told him I could not spare him the time to talk any longer – could I catch up with him sometime? 'You can call on me any time you want,' he replied breezily. 'I'm on permanent sick leave from work.'

That was just mildly amusing, but there were others who were downright offensive.

One man arrived on my doorstep at 9pm on a Saturday night. I had met him at a couple of Christian meetings in the past, and now he told me that he had heard about my wife. He explained that God had given him a message that he was compelled to deliver to me. With the fervour of a man who knows he is right, he told me that my wife was sick because there was sin in my ministry. If I repented of whatever I had done wrong, Edrie would be healed instantly.

Now when tough things invade your life, it is not wrong to ask the question: 'Is God trying to grab my attention?' I had searched my own heart and asked that very question several times, but had concluded that Edrie's illness was not some kind of divine wake-up call. When I told the man this, he seemed a little sceptical, then adjusted his position: 'I might have got it slightly wrong. Maybe there isn't sin in your life. Maybe it is some secret undiscovered sin in your wife's life, and, if she repents, God will heal her.'

That's when I hit him.

Well, I didn't – but it was a close-run thing.

When 'theology' doesn't help

I'm not telling the story above to show that Christians should never tell you difficult things when you are suffering. Sometimes that's exactly what you need, and the 'wounds from a friend' (Proverbs 27:6) can be a great blessing. What was wrong here was that this guy did not know me or my circumstances. More than that, he had built his advice on a faulty and destructive theology, at the basis of which was a view of God that insisted it is never his will that any of his people should suffer. If they do, it is not part of his plan, meaning the fault must lie elsewhere. Either they have some hidden sin or they do not have enough faith to tip the balance and let God come to their rescue with miraculous healing. Sometimes, the problem is even more sinister and some mysterious demonic involvement is suggested.

Theologies like this come from what is sometimes known as the 'Prosperity Gospel'. God always wants his people to prosper in body and mind and circumstances. Christians should never experience hardships, and, if they do, the fault lies with them, not with God.

What is never permitted by people who espouse this theory is that this person may love God and be trusting in his goodness, and yet be sick because that is what God in his kindness has sent into their lives. Like all bad theology, this theory is incredibly destructive. Instead of giving comfort and consolation to a vulnerable person, it leaves them wondering what on earth they have done wrong. Or it may cause them to agonize over how they might build up their faith to miracle-working proportions, believing that without such high-level faith, a willing deity is powerless to come to our aid. At a time when you need to know more than ever that you can trust God to work all things together for your ultimate good, you are left confused and uncertain.

Meet Job

It is clear we have to clear the decks of some false ideas about suffering. To do this, we will turn to one of the oldest books in the world, the book of Job.

This ancient book has comforted Christians for hundreds of years. When Edrie first became ill, I found myself dwelling in Job and the Psalms. They put into words what I was feeling but was unable to articulate.

The book of Job begins with an open secret. Three times we are told that Job was 'blameless and upright; he feared God and shunned evil' (1:1, 8; 2:3). It is clear right from the start that his suffering is not the result of any secret or unconscious sin on his part. Job is a good guy. He is also incredibly wealthy (1:2–3) and has a large family – a sign of blessing in an ancient culture (1:2–5).

The heavenly court

Then we get a peek of the heavenly court where God boasts to Satan about the integrity of his servant Job. The devil's riposte is that this is just a matter of enlightened self-interest. 'Does Job fear God for nothing?' (Job 1:9). He means that any person who has prospered and been protected like Job is bound to be grateful. Only a fool would risk this highly favoured position by compromising his integrity (1:10–11). In other words, Job is a good guy because of the fringe benefits.

In order to prove the devil wrong, God lets him inflict two waves of suffering on Job (1:12).

Firstly, using bands of marauding desert brigands and natural phenomena like fire from heaven and a mighty wind, all Job's possessions are removed and his sons and daughters slaughtered (1:13–19). But this only stimulates Job's faith:

> The LORD gave and the LORD has taken away;
>   may the name of the LORD be praised.
> (1:21)

In a second wave, the devil attacks Job's health, and he is left with a painful and disfiguring skin disease (2:6–8). Even his wife advises him to abandon his trust in God and ditch his integrity by cursing God (2:9). Again, Job expresses his faith in God. The author affirms, 'In all this, Job did not sin in what he said' (2:10).

With friends like these . . .

It is at this point that three friends appear. When they first see Job, they are utterly shocked – they can barely recognize him (2:11–12).

Their first response is great. They don't preach at him or try to come up with a pat answer – they grieve with him and sit in the dust where he is sitting and keeping silent for seven days (2:12–13). We too know that there are times when we need silent love rather than bland platitudes or half-baked theology.

So far, so good.

Then Job speaks. He mourns over the intensity of his suffering and the profound darkness which seems to press around him:

> Why is light given to those in misery,
>   and life to the bitter of soul?
> (3:20)

> Why is life given to a man
>   whose way is hidden,
>   whom God has hedged in?
> (3:23)

His words are extreme, a kind of primal scream from the heart of a man at the edge of endurance. He has lost everything except his life, and every second he lives is agony.

I underlined these words in my Bible. I can remember reading them one long night when sleep would not come. Instead of sharing my bed, Edrie was far away and all alone and vulnerable. I don't think I was angry with God – more than anything, I was confused and desperate. The experience seemed to be contrary to everything I had learned about God during my twenty years of being a Christian. Like Job, I felt that God had hedged me in, and there was no escape.

It is at this point that the friends weigh in.

Eliphaz, Bildad and Zophar listen to what Job is saying, and then respond to him. We run through this 'dialogue in the dark' three times. Each time they articulate a kind of 'retribution theology': they say that people only suffer in this way as a direct consequence of personal and deliberate sin. This is rigid and mechanical, and only becomes more strident in response to Job's protestations of innocence (4:7–11; 11:13–20).

Job does not claim to be sinless (9:2), but he protests that he is not receiving justice from God (9:21–24). Why is God treating him this way?

Faith in dark places

Even as he confesses his confusion, there are moments when Job's faith seems to rise above his circumstances. He may complain to God, but he will not surrender his faith (Job 13:15). He believes that his suffering is purposeful and will come to an end:

> But he [God] knows the way that I take;
>> when he has tested me, I shall come forth as gold.
> (23:10)

In words that point forwards to the ministry of Christ, he confesses:

> Even now my witness is in heaven;
>> my advocate is on high.
> My intercessor is my friend
>> as my eyes pour out tears to God;
> on behalf of a man he pleads with God
>> as one pleads for a friend.
> (16:19–21)

He also expresses the hope of a life beyond the grave:

> I know that my Redeemer lives,
>> and that in the end he will stand on the earth.
> And after my skin has been destroyed,
>> yet in my flesh I will see God;
> I myself will see him
>> with my own eyes – I, and not another.
>> How my heart yearns within me!
> (19:25–27)

It seems to me that this hovering between hope and despair is the very thing that confirms the authenticity of the book of Job, making it so helpful. Isn't this exactly our experience when we suffer? One minute our faith seems to have disappeared without trace; the next, it has risen as if from nowhere and is singing in the darkness.

So the friends fail to persuade Job that his suffering is the result of his sin (32:5), and at this point a new character, Elihu, speaks (32 – 37).

Elihu is a bit of an enigma. He is a younger man who claims to be able to teach Job wisdom, if only he will listen (33:33). He sets forth the same theology of retribution (34:11, 25–27, 37), but he also seems to suggest that suffering can have a purpose (33:17, 28).

The voice of God

It is only at this point that God enters the fray.

Job has longed to meet with God (23:2–7), and now God answers out of the storm. He does not reply to Job's questions, but rebukes him for doubting his justice (40:8). The essence of the response is that human understanding is finite, while divine wisdom is infinite. It is impossible for Job to comprehend God's ways (38:2–3). The infinite God knows what Job could never know (38:1 – 40:5) and does what Job could never do (40:6 – 41:34).

Job submits to God's sovereignty and wisdom (42:1–6), and in the last chapter of the book, he is reconciled to God and his prosperity is restored. He may have argued with God and questioned his providences, but he did not 'curse God and die' (Job 2:9). His very lamentations are proof that he is convinced of the ultimate justice of God. Only someone convinced that God is wise and fair would struggle as Job does when circumstances seem to prove otherwise.

The restoration proves the ultimate justice of God in a world where Jesus Christ had not yet brought life and immortality to light. The end of the book should be seen as the old-covenant way in which God vindicates his people and establishes justice. The new-covenant perspective does not promise such vindication in this life, but looks for a better vindication beyond the grave. Sometimes, even Job's faith seems to look beyond this life (19:25–27).

So how does the book of Job help us to clear the decks of false and misleading theology?

I think we have three lessons to learn.

1. Living in a dangerous world

Our first lesson is that the causes of suffering are complex. How did Job's suffering come upon him? It is clear that there were visible and immediately discernible causes of his misfortune. Job suffered because of the rapacious greed of his neighbours, because of a series of natural disasters and because of a mysterious disease that invaded his body.

The Sabeans and Chaldeans – two groups of ancient marauding bandits – stole his oxen and donkeys and carried off his camels, slaughtering all his servants in the process (1:13–15, 17). Then, fire from heaven (probably lightning) destroyed his sheep and the servants tending them (1:16). Finally came the hardest blow of all: a mighty desert wind blew down the house where his children were feasting and killed all of them (1:18–20). All this was followed by a particularly painful viral infection, disfiguring Job and leaving him almost unrecognizable as he sat in the ashes of his broken life (2:7–8, 12).

All of these causes can be given scientific or psychological explanations. A meteorologist might have been able to predict the lightning and the desert wind. A criminal psychologist could have analysed the motivation of the nomadic terrorists who stole Job's possessions and left death and destruction in their wake. A consultant dermatologist might have been able to take a skin sample and diagnose Job's disease.

But would they have been able to give a satisfactory explanation of what happened to Job? Yes and no. Clearly, these things were immediately responsible for what took place. Natural phenomena have natural explanations. Even freak weather conditions can be seen, with hindsight, to have natural causes. If Job had been able to receive weather forecasts and take precautions, he might have been able to protect his family from this ancient hurricane Katrina. The wicked men who had invaded his property were motivated by greed and were criminally responsible for their actions. Advances in medical science may well have led to the correct diagnosis and treatment of Job's disease.

So there are natural causes for natural phenomena. And we too live in a real world of cause and effect.

When Edrie became ill, I wanted to find the very best medical treatment available. I knew that she was in God's hands, but I was also so grateful that God had sent some pretty skilful neurologists to help. It would be an act of gross stupidity, ingratitude and arrogance to refuse medical help because we thought it betrayed a lack of faith.

Praise God and keep taking the tablets.

An enemy has done this

At the same time, we have looked behind the scenes and we know that there is more to this than meets the eye. In Job's suffering, we cannot ignore the part played by the mysterious and malevolent figure of Satan. He is the immediate instigator of this suffering (1:12), and it is he who afflicts Job with painful sores (2:4–7).

What are we to make of this? Clearly, the Bible takes seriously the existence of a personal and powerful force of evil in the universe. The devil appears in the third chapter of Genesis as the tempter set on ruining God's beautiful new world. Jesus described him as a murderer and liar from the beginning. The devil inhabits the pages of the Bible until his final judgment and expulsion to the lake of fire (Revelation 20:7–10).

Some years ago, I remember hearing Rabbi Lionel Blue sharing a 'Thought for the Day' on Radio 4.[1] He was speculating about the nature of evil, and mentioned a guard in a Nazi concentration camp. This man had a glass eye. Indeed, it was almost indistinguishable from the real eye. How could you tell the difference? The glass eye was the one with the hint of pity in it!

His point, as you may have guessed, was that some people are so consumed with malevolence and hatred that they have closed their hearts to any manifestation of mercy.

I always think of the devil when I remember that story. He is driven by a hatred of all that God has created, and this is seen in his wild and vindictive attempt to hurt or damage or destroy anything that is precious to God. He attacks Job both because he hates him and because he wants to prove that God's trust in his servant is misplaced. In doing this, he appears to exert a certain amount of control over natural phenomena, over wicked men and even over the microscopic organisms that invade Job's body. It is no wonder that he is called 'the god of this world' and 'the prince of the power of the air'. Even Jesus seemed to acknowledge that some diseases might have a satanic origin (Matthew 17:14–19).

However, we must not go too far. If we read Job carefully, we discover that the devil is on a tight rein. He protests that he cannot touch Job because God has put a protective hedge around him (1:10). Even when God allows Satan to attack Job's family and possessions, he puts an embargo on any attack on Job's health (1:12). When that embargo is lifted and God puts Job into Satan's hands, he is forbidden to take Job's life (2:6). Yes, Satan has power, but it is limited to what God allows. He is only serving God's purposes. He is, to use Martin Luther's phrase, 'only God's devil'.[2] Job recognizes that it is God who has given and taken away his blessings (1:21), and after Job 2, the devil is never mentioned again. When God finally answers Job, he does not tell him that it was the devil who caused his suffering. God takes full responsibility for what has happened. The devil is a minor character who has served God's purposes and then left the stage. In God's script for the universe, the devil is only a minor character who cannot deviate from the role allotted to him.

In the hands of God

This leads us to the ultimate cause of Job's agony. Job is in the hands of God, the One who both orchestrates and controls the test. The final vision of God is of One who is unrivalled in power and authority. It was God who laid the earth's foundations and marked off its dimensions. It was God who set the sea behind doors and shaped the earth like clay under a seal. It is God who stocks the storehouses of snow and hail and reserves them for days of battle. He adorns himself with glory and splendour, and clothes himself in honour and majesty. Clearly, God is in ultimate control over everything in his universe – from natural phenomena and weather conditions to human beings and demonic forces.

Similarly, when we suffer, we are in the hands of a gracious and loving Father. The idea that this God would like to help his suffering children, but that his hands are tied until his children manage to drum up enough faith to tip the balance, is both unhelpful and untrue.

God may use secondary causes; in fact he usually does. Satan may be weaving his malevolent webs when we suffer, but only to the extent that God allows it. It may cause some confusion and even consternation – think of all Job's protestations – but, finally, in our Father's hands is the best place to be.

To be honest, during the last twenty years there have been times when my faith has seemed frail and fragile and almost ready to collapse. I have struggled with seeing my wife stripped of her dignity and reduced by her agony. I have doubted all kinds of things. I have got angry. I have exploded and lashed out. I do not like what is happening to my sweetheart one little bit. Chronic illness never goes away. Sometimes I find myself asking, 'Come on, realistically, how much more can we take?'

But one thing I have never doubted is that, in the darkest

circumstances, we were only ever in the hands of God. That has been the ultimate source of comfort and hope.

2. The nightmare of false theologies

The second lesson we need to learn from Job is that the theology of retribution is simplistic and misleading and downright wrong.

As mentioned above, Job's friends are initially very sympathetic – they sit where he sits and weep with him. But, having listened to his lament, they then make the mistake of opening their mouths.

The theology they articulate could have come out of the mouth of my Saturday-night caller at the beginning of this chapter. Instead of comforting Job, they cast themselves as the prosecution counsel. Like my visitor, they probably mean to help. However, they have a rigid and unbending view of life which leaves no room for innocent suffering.

Listen to Eliphaz:

> Consider now: who, being innocent, has ever perished?
>> Where were the upright ever destroyed?
> As I have observed, those who plough evil
>> and those who sow trouble reap it.
> (4:7–8)

Bildad chips in:

> How long will you say such things?
>> Your words are a blustering wind.
> Does God pervert justice?
>> Does the Almighty pervert what is right?
> When your children sinned against him,
>> he gave them over to the penalty of their sin.
> (8:2–4)

What about Zophar?

> Are all these words to go unanswered?
>> Is this talker to be vindicated?
> Will your idle talk reduce others to silence?
>> Will no one rebuke you when you mock? . . .
> Oh, how I wish that God would speak,
>> that he would open his lips against you
> and disclose to you the secrets of wisdom,
>> for true wisdom has two sides.
>> Know this: God has even forgotten some of your sin.
> (11:2–3, 5–6)

There you have it. You are only suffering because of your own deliberate and unacknowledged sin. Or maybe it is because your kids sinned. In fact, God has even forgotten some of your sins – if he remembered the lot, you would be suffering even more than you are suffering now. If I were Job, I'd want to scream back, 'How would that work? How could I possibly suffer more than I am suffering now?!'

But the friends are relentless. The more he states his innocence, the more they insist on their rigid theology of retribution.

Where they got it wrong

Of course, there is a strong connection between sin and suffering. Suffering entered the world because of Adam's sin. It is also true that often our suffering is the direct result of our wrong decisions. However, if the book of Job teaches us anything, it is that a rigid and unimaginative theology of retribution will not fit every case.

From the outset, we've known that Job is a good man who fears God and hates evil. When he protests his innocence, he is only agreeing with God's verdict on his life (1:8; 2:3). Job says some stupid things in the heated dialogue, but then who wouldn't? In the final chapters, God says to the friends casting themselves in the role of his spokesmen, 'I am angry with you . . .

because you have not spoken the truth about me, as my servant Job has' (42:7). Their theology is crooked (42:7–8), and they must ask Job to pray for them so that they will not be punished for their folly (42:8). God vindicates Job by restoring his fortunes (42:12–17).

The lesson is surely clear. Innocent people do suffer. When tragedy invades our lives, it is far too simplistic to assume we have done something wrong and God is paying us back for our mistakes.

During those first few weeks of Edrie's illness, I kept coming back to this. The devil tried to bully me into thinking that Edrie or I had done something wrong to bring suffering crashing down on us. Twenty years later, he still tries the same tactic. When I am vulnerable, I listen to him – maybe you do as well? There are plenty of false guides out there who support his accusations. But these are lies. We are not necessarily deaf rebels on the road to disaster, with God trying to gain our attention. Sometimes, we can be doing our best to serve God faithfully, and our world falls apart. It happened to Job. It can happen to us today.

So why does God allow it? This leads us to our final lesson from Job.

3. The wisdom of humility

The third lesson we need to learn is the wisdom of humility. This flows from God's answer to Job at the end of the book. There are some mysteries we cannot understand and some enigmas we have to leave in God's hands. The three friends set out an unbending theology that allows no room for mystery. Job asks for simple answers. But in the end, there is no simple answer.

Instead, God bombards Job with a series of questions designed to make him realize there are some things we just cannot comprehend (Job 38 – 42). If Job cannot understand how God *made* the world, how can he ever hope to understand how he *runs* the world? In the end, we have to learn to live with mystery. We walk by faith, not by explanations.

Job comes to look at life in a different way:

> My ears had heard of you
>> but now my eyes have seen you.
> Therefore I despise myself
>> and repent in dust and ashes.
> (42:5–6)

One of the most comforting things that Edrie and I have come to learn is that we don't have to understand everything God is doing in order to trust him. There have been times when I have watched my beautiful wife struggling with simple things and have inwardly shouted at God. 'Why have you allowed this? Please explain it to me!' And there have been a whole host of reasons that have made sense and helped us to cope. But in the end, we come back to this great truth: God is God and his ways are mysterious. Simplistic theological answers are almost always wrong. It is better to trust God in the darkness than to seek consolation in a false theology that claims to offer help but ends in confusion and despair.

We walk by faith, not by explanations.

In the New Testament, God embraces human suffering and demonstrates that, in the midst of the horror of the cross, his wisdom can be clearly seen (1 Corinthians 1:18–25). In the light of the cross, it is possible to suffer and yet go on loving and trusting God in the darkness. We will turn our thoughts and attention to this highly significant angle on suffering in chapter 11.

3. A word from another world

Meet Jonah

A long time before Edrie fell ill, I was going through a particularly stressful time in my ministry, so my kids bought me a goldfish for my birthday. Edrie had put them up to it. She had heard somewhere that watching fish swim around a bowl can be incredibly relaxing. You forget your troubles as you watch your piscine friend doing the circuit of his tiny aquatic world.

I decided to give it a go.

I called him Jonah (although this story does not have anything to do with his namesake) and we developed quite a relationship. Every morning, I would feed him and chat about the day ahead. Before I went to bed, I would check up on him. I felt a growing affection for him and was convinced that, every time I appeared above his bowl, he was swimming to greet me with a smile on his face. (Can goldfish smile?)

Then came the devastating news. I was listening to the car radio and they were interviewing an expert on tropical fish. He informed a listening world that goldfish have a memory span of about three minutes. They can remember nothing beyond that.

It appeared that every encounter with Jonah was a first time for him.

I have since discovered that this is something of a myth. Researchers at St Andrew's University have found that gold-fish are at least as intelligent as rats. Their memory span may be significantly longer than three minutes.[1] But the point remains the same – they have little comprehension of the world we live in.

In any case, it's not very exciting being a goldfish, but at least you are always getting to meet new people!

Even greater gap

So why the Jonah story?

I came to realize that there was a massive gap between my mind and the mind of this little fish. He was confined to his small and uneventful world, bounded by a glass bowl. My world is so much bigger, and involves space and time and memory and experiences that even the most advanced creature cannot share. Jonah could never even begin to understand my world.

But what about the gap between my mind and the mind of God? Surely it is even greater? Of course, I have been created in the image of God, with the ability and capacity to relate person-ally to my Creator. But there is such a huge disparity between my mind and the mind of the One who spoke the whole of creation into existence that it is not surprising that some of the things he does are beyond my feeble comprehension.

That was the lesson that Job had to learn, as we saw in the previous chapter. It is a lesson we all still have to learn today.

If that was all we could offer on the subject, we might find ourselves floundering about, unable to share anything meaning-ful about pain. But there is more to say. At the end of the book, God answered Job out of the whirlwind. It was God's voice and the words he spoke that transformed the situation. And that voice is still able to transform our circumstances today.

The most precious thing in the universe

I became a Christian when I was eleven and can hardly remember a time when I did not trust that the Bible was God's Word. For my twelfth birthday, my auntie bought me a zip-up Bible, and, until it fell apart many years later, it was my most treasured possession. I remember my youth leader saying to us, 'Boys, trust the book; it's God's book, and he means what he says. It's the most precious treasure in the universe.' He told us that he loved to see well-read, well-thumbed Bibles, so I went home and screwed mine up to give the impression of constant use! One of the things I loved about Edrie was that she also loved the Bible. When I became a preacher, she became my most faithful and perceptive critic, and woe betide me if I strayed from the Word!

It was during Edrie's long weeks in hospital that the Bible became more and more precious to both of us. What we found in it during those dark days sustained us, and, when we read it together, we heard Jesus' voice and saw his face and felt the force of his promises. Here we recognized the voice of the Good Shepherd (John 10:14–16).

Evangelical Christians are sometimes accused of worshipping the Bible. This is not true. We worship one triune God: Father, Son and Holy Spirit. However, we love and honour the Bible because, in it, we hear the voice of the God we love. Through his Word, God nourishes our souls and gives us the grace to persevere.

The voice of the skies

We can see this in Psalm 19.

We don't know when David wrote this Psalm, but, at some point in his tempestuous life, he was clearly overwhelmed by the majesty of God's creation. As he meditated on the magnificence of the skies, he looked beyond them to their Creator:

The heavens declare the glory of God;
　　the skies proclaim the work of his hands.
(Psalm 19:1)

God is not silent.

God speaks clearly and constantly and universally

God speaks so clearly and unmistakably that this creation is said to 'pour forth speech' (Psalm 19:2). It is like a fountain that never ceases to bubble up and overflow. This is no vague or obscure whisper. In letters a million miles high, God has inscribed his glory across the canvas of the cosmos.

He speaks constantly. From the beginning of time until time shall cease, this voice has sounded out and will sound out (19:2). At night, we have the evidence of a billion twinkling stars. During the day, we feel the heat of the sun which moves across the sky in stately grandeur, like a bridegroom riding out to claim his bride or Usain Bolt burning up the track (19:4–6).

He speaks universally (19:3–4). On mountains and on scattered islands, he is heard. In deserts and across mighty oceans, he speaks. In forests and in the middle of great cities, he does not keep silent. This voice speaks one universal and comprehensive language. Human beings can ignore it, but they cannot say they have not heard it.

So what does God say in creation?

At the very least, it is a clear and present reminder of the fact that he is there. One of my earliest memories as a child was of a Robinson Crusoe picture book. On the cover, there was a picture of Robinson on the beach, dressed in grass skirt, grass hat and grass shoes, and carrying a grass parasol. But what really stands out is the amazement on his face as he looks down at a footprint in the sand left by someone else. It is proof that there is at least one other person on the island he had thought was uninhabited.

God has left his fingerprints all over the universe. You don't need the latest gadgets from CSI to detect the existence of a

Creator. Later, Paul will say that, since the creation of the world, God's invisible qualities – his eternal power and divine nature – have been clearly seen, so that people are without excuse (Romans 1:19–20).

The word 'awesome' is somewhat overused today, but when we think about the voice of the skies, it seems an entirely appropriate word to use. Our little planet is the third rock from the sun in a solar system which is part of the Milky Way, the galaxy to which we belong. On a clear night, you may be able to see a couple of thousand stars with the naked eye, but, in the Milky Way alone, there are a hundred billion stars. How do we even compute such a number? If you wanted to count to a hundred billion and you began at this moment to count one number per second, it would take you three thousand years before you had finished. And the Milky Way is only one of one hundred billion galaxies.[2] Wow! Surely the greatest understatement in the Bible must be Genesis 1:16: 'He [God] also made the stars.'

Too big to care?

When an eminent cosmologist was asked if he believed in God, he is reported to have said that such a question is not suitable for a physicist. However, if God did exist, one thing we could be certain of is that he would know nothing about us. We are such tiny, insignificant beings on a little rock at the edge of an average-sized galaxy in the middle of nowhere.

But that's not what the Bible says. The One who 'determines the number of the stars and calls them each by name' is also the One who 'heals the broken-hearted and binds up their wounds' (Psalm 147:3–4). He has not washed his hands of his creation. Instead, he has rolled up his sleeves and, in the person of his Son, has entered the world he has made. The Creator of a billion spinning galaxies became smaller than a full stop in the womb of the Virgin Mary (John 1:14). He does know and care about us, and he even comes to heal our broken hearts.

God is like the conductor of some great orchestra. He controls every instrument before him, producing sublime music. But when his son stumbles onto the stage with a cut knee, he takes him in his arms and, without ceasing to conduct the orchestra, comforts his unhappy child. We come to God with our broken hearts, and, without pausing, he continues to conduct the symphony of the stars while sweeping us into his arms and whispering that he loves us and that all is well.

I remember a night several years after the onset of Edrie's illness. Edrie had been struggling with pain that had robbed her of her sleep. Before dawn, she had finally gone off, and at this point I had set off for a walk to clear my mind. I cried out to God and asked him to give us the grace we needed to survive. I couldn't read my Bible because it was too dark. But I could look up into the sky and see thousands of stars scattered like diamonds on black velvet. Suddenly, I was overwhelmed with a sense of the greatness of the mighty Creator who was also my loving Father. I could trust him with my sweetheart.

Hearing the voice of God makes all the difference.

The voice of the Scriptures

But David doesn't leave it there.

In the second part of the Psalm (19:7–9), he begins to describe another way in which God speaks to us:

> The law of the LORD is perfect,
>   refreshing the soul.
> The statutes of the LORD are trustworthy,
>   making wise the simple.
> (19:7)

David turns from the voice of the stars to the voice of the Scriptures. He now speaks with a new warmth and intimacy. He goes on to describe the Word of God in his hands as 'more precious than gold' and as 'sweeter than honey' (19:10). Why is this? Because, although the creation is a clear voice pointing to the existence of a glorious Creator, the skies do not tell us that God loves us. The majestic mountains do not assure us that God cares for us: the tempestuous oceans do not whisper that God will send his Son to die for us. For these things, we need a surer and more familiar voice.

In the Bible, God speaks to our hearts and unfolds the nature of his heart. Here is God's love letter to all who will read it. Here, God speaks to us personally and invites us to trust him.

A word from another world

David tells us three things about the Bible.

Firstly, he assures us that this really is God speaking. Six times in these verses he affirms the divine authorship of Scripture. God used human authors like David and Moses and Peter and Paul, but Scripture is also 'the very words of God' (Romans 3:2). It is the 'law of the LORD', the 'statutes of the LORD', the 'precepts of the LORD', the 'commands of the LORD', the 'fear of the LORD' and the 'decrees of the LORD' (Psalm 19:7–9). The Bible bears the clear marks of human authorship and is, at the same time, 'a word from another world'. We can approach it with the confidence that what the Bible says is what God says. Paul tells us that all Scripture is 'God-breathed' (2 Timothy 3:16).

Secondly, David describes the character of Scripture. If the Bible really is God speaking, we would expect it to be reliable and trustworthy. The God of the Bible loves to delight us with the certainty and security of his promises. He is the God on whose word we can depend. This is what we expect and this David affirms.

The word God speaks is 'perfect', 'trustworthy', 'right', 'radiant', 'pure' and 'sure'. David is clearly affirming the reliability of Scripture. When troubled souls turn to the Bible, they find a book with promises on which they can stake their whole lives:

The words of the LORD are flawless,
>   like silver purified in a crucible,
>   like gold refined seven times.
(Psalm 12:6)

When David thinks of God's words being tested and tried, he is not really thinking about those who cast doubts on the authenticity of Scripture. Critics come and critics go, but the Word of the Lord endures forever. What David really has in mind is the way in which the trials of life test the promises and commitments that God has made. His conclusion is that, no matter what intense experiences of suffering we may go through, God's promises will always prove to be true. When the promises are thrown into the furnace of affliction, they will shine even more brightly.

Thirdly, David reminds us of the power of the Word of God. It changes lives. It revives flagging souls and it makes simple people wise. It gives joy to grieving hearts and light to those who feel as if they are in utter darkness. Again, this should not surprise us. God spoke the whole universe into existence by the power of his Word, and it is his Word that continues to keep it in existence. Jesus Christ is the eternal Word become flesh. When he speaks, storms are stilled and crowds are amazed and the dead hear their name and rise from the grave. The Word of God transforms the darkest situation, flooding it with light.

When the promises are thrown into the furnace of affliction, they will shine even more brightly.

As a pastor, I have seen this happen hundreds of times. I think of the man dying of a painful disease whose last days were filled with confidence that the grave was conquered – a confidence nourished by promises of hope scattered like jewels throughout the Bible. I think of the childless couple who have come to terms with their empty home and empty arms because God has promised to sustain them and give them grace to sing his praises, even with tears in their eyes. I think of the bereaved mum who will never fully recover from her broken heart, but who has suddenly discovered that, when she reads the Bible, it is more precious to her than ever before.

Only God speaking in his Word can do this.

The voice of the servant

In the last section of Psalm 19, David describes his own response to the Bible (19:10–14). He was no armchair theologian. Indeed, his life reads like a Hollywood blockbuster. Look at the psalms he wrote and you will discover that he experienced the whole gamut of human emotions. He knew what it was to be slandered, reviled and misrepresented; he experienced physical danger and the terrible pain of bereavement; he was so sick that it seemed that the sickness was unto death, and he tasted the crushing agony of a guilty conscience. Many of the psalms were written out of these experiences. What sustained him? The promises in God's Word. That was why, in the last part of the psalm (19:10–14), he affirmed how precious the words of Scripture were to him:

> They are more precious than gold,
>   than much pure gold;
> they are sweeter than honey,
>   than honey from the honeycomb.
> (Psalm 19:10)

The king of Israel whose vaults were filled with gold recognized their tawdry magnificence when compared to the golden words God had spoken. God's promises make us rich with a wealth that is unsurpassed. Or to follow the psalm's change of metaphors, these same words are more precious than the sweetest things that this world can ever offer.

The living Word of God both warns and rewards the servant of God who listens and puts it into practice (19:11). Scripture acts as a kind of early-warning system, designed to protect us from sin (19:12–13). There is a kind of gravity to sin: if you get too close to the edge, you suddenly find yourself plummeting to unexpected depths. The warnings of the Bible should ring a bell in our consciences and tell us we are in danger. The Bible is precious because it protects us from being shipwrecked.

When John Wesley went to Oxford University, his mother wrote in the front of his Bible: 'Either this book will keep you from sin or sin will keep you from this book.'[3]

The psalm ends with a prayer (19:14). David wants God's Word to shape his words and thoughts, so that he may please God.

Light in our darkness

This world is a place of trial and danger and perplexity. Unexpected things invade our lives and kick us, even when we're down. Like a confused and bewildered little goldfish, we stare out at the chaotic cosmos that sometimes makes no sense at all, and where God's ways sometimes can seem obtuse or down-right nonsensical.

In such a situation, we need guidance from another world. We don't need an exhaustive explanation of every little turn in the road, but some clarity about the big picture of what God is doing to guide us. We also need the calm assurance that all is well, and that God still loves us and is too wise to make mistakes and too kind to cause us unnecessary pain. In the Bible, we have access to objective, infallible and authoritative truth. We open the book and know we are reading the promises of our Rock and our Redeemer. Once we have interpreted them correctly, we can rely on them totally. We do not live by explanations; we live by promises.

The voice that brings comfort

My dad became a Christian at fifty and died of cancer on the eve of his sixty-first birthday.

I could not have asked for a better dad. When I came home aged eleven and told him I had become a Christian, he wasn't quite sure what to make of it, but not once did he put a stumbling block in the way of my faith. He was present when I was baptized and he began to take an interest in Christianity after I had been a follower of Jesus for about five years. In my first year at university, he came to visit and I gave him a Christian book to read on the coach back to Birmingham. Two days later, he sent me a letter:

'I read that book you gave me. It was great. When I got home, I went up to my room and knelt by my bed and asked Jesus to be my Saviour. Is that OK?'

OK? Not half! I jumped for joy.

For ten years, he was a faithful disciple of Jesus Christ, growing in leaps and bounds. He served as a deacon in the church where Edrie and I had first met. He grew more quickly in his love for God and his desire to know him and serve him than anyone I had ever known.

And then cancer struck. Doctors opened him up and found there was nothing they could do. He had six months to live.

I spent the last hours with him, and he asked me to read the Scriptures to him and tell him about Jesus. He was getting weaker, but those hours were precious beyond imagination. He kept thanking me for introducing him to the Saviour. He asked me to describe heaven. He spoke of his love for Jesus who had saved him even though he had neglected him for most of his life. He wept as, at his request, I read the accounts of the cross. 'It was for me! It was for me!' he kept repeating. In the words of one of the Puritans, 'God put heaven in his soul before he put his soul in heaven.'

Where did that strength and faith come from?

Dad worked nights in the flavour stores at the Cadbury Chocolate Factory. In the long watches of those nights, when there was nothing else to do and the other blokes were playing cards, Dad read his Bible. When he died, I inherited it. It was unique in two ways. Firstly, when you opened its pages, it smelled of chocolate! Secondly, Dad had written all over it. In the middle of the night, the great Creator of the universe, who was my dad's heavenly Father, had spoken clearly and warmly to his son. Dad had put the date next to every verse and every passage where God had met him and nourished the faith he had discovered late in life. The date was often accompanied with three letters in bold print: PTL, for 'Praise the Lord'.

If you had asked my dad, who left school at fourteen and never passed an exam in his life, whether he thought the Bible was true, he would have said, 'Of course it is. I don't know how I could live without it.' As Christians, we are not supposed to live without it. When you live in the middle of the book, you need a word from another world to sustain you. You need promises to brighten your darkness. You soon discover that man 'does not live on bread alone but on every word that comes from the mouth of God'.[4]

4. Living in a broken world

I love cemeteries – I always have done.

There is something strangely calming about the place where the dead sleep. I often go to the cemetery to think or read, or even to pray. You are rarely disturbed – occasionally someone comes and digs a hole – but most of the time you are left to your own devices. For the Mallards, no holiday is complete without a cemetery visit. A couple of years ago, we were up in the beautiful city of Glasgow, and I discovered that they had a huge cemetery in the outskirts. It was actually called a 'necropolis' or city of the dead. I wanted to spend the day there. Edrie wasn't so sure, but then, being in a wheelchair, she goes where she is taken!

I have to say that the place blew me away. There were some newer graves, but also huge ancient tombs surrounded by rusting iron railings. I found myself wondering whether there might be a little Glaswegian cemetery attendant somewhere who had a key that would fit the ancient rust-encrusted locks. And if they did have a key, would it even work any more? What a contrast with the risen Christ who has the keys of death and Hades hanging at his belt (Revelation 1:17–18). One day, every gate, even the gates of death, will yield to him.

There's another reason why I love cemeteries. I love to read the inscriptions. Look at the graves of those who were buried a hundred years ago, and you notice two things.

One is the warmth of the sentiments. Promises are frequently made that a dear daughter or a beloved husband or precious parents will never be forgotten. The second thing is that, ironically, the graves are almost always neglected and overgrown and forgotten.

It makes you realize how transient human life is. A few years ago, these same people loved and were loved. They enjoyed the sun on their faces and the wind in their hair. They left footprints in the sands of time, but, to mix our metaphors, the winds of change have blown over them and left no memory, except perhaps for the most committed genealogist.

And in a hundred years' time, we too will be where they are. It may be sobering but it is utterly realistic. We live in a world where:

> Time, like an ever-rolling stream,
> Bears all its sons away;
> They fly forgotten, as a dream
> Dies at the opening day.[1]

I am reminded of a joke I once heard about an undertaker who signed his letter not 'yours faithfully' but 'yours eventually'.

Death is our ultimate enemy as we live in the middle of the book. Only at the end will death be defeated.

The psalm of Moses

Psalm 90 was written by Moses at the end of the forty years that Israel had spent wandering round in the wilderness. The people of Israel had left Egypt with such high hopes. God had rescued them and had promised to give them a land flowing with milk and honey. When they reached Mount Sinai, they willingly pledged themselves to be utterly faithful to him. But within forty days, they had committed spiritual adultery, worshipping the golden calf and going wild at the foot of the mountain where Moses was meeting with God (Exodus 32). God was amazingly gracious to them and did not wipe them out.

That should have been a warning, but in a short time they were rebelling against God at the oasis town of Kadesh Barnea on the edge of the Land of Promise (Numbers 13 – 14). The result? God declared that all those who had rebelled would perish outside the Promised Land.

Moses saw a whole generation – perhaps half a million people – die in the wilderness over the next forty years. So many funerals, so many graves. If you have ever seen the rows upon rows of white crosses in the cemeteries of Flanders Fields, you will have some idea of how this must have felt.

In this psalm, Moses contemplates human mortality and sets it within the context of the experiences of the people who rebelled in the wilderness. This psalm consists of a meditation (1–6), an explanation (7–11) and an application (12–16).

From everlasting to everlasting

Moses begins with a confession of confidence. Amid all the changing scenes of life, God has remained the faithful unchanging refuge of his people. He has been their dwelling-place (90:1). Life is like a shadow moving swiftly across the ground, and the one stable, unchangeable reality is the God who invites his people to trust him: our rock, our fortress and our strong deliverer.

Moses then begins to meditate on the difference between God and human beings (90:2–6). God was present from the beginning of creation – before the ancient mountains were born. Indeed, Moses takes us to a time *before* creation: God is from everlasting to everlasting.

What does this mean?

It is difficult to put into words. A famous American comedian quipped, in answer to the question, 'What is eternity?', 'It is a very long time, particularly towards the end.'[2]

But of course, eternity by definition can have neither beginning nor end. The whole of time, from the creation of the world until the formation of the new heaven and the new earth, is, from God's point of view, just a brief episode in eternity. Imagine two massive circles that only overlap slightly. One represents eternity past and the other eternity future. The tiny area where they touch, hard to see and difficult to measure, represents the whole history of this universe that we call home.

Before creation, this one God existed as three persons (Trinity) in loving fellowship and cloudless communion. The Father and the Son and the Holy Spirit delighted in each other, existing together in blissful and joyful companionship. And yet, amazingly, there came a time when the eternal Son of God left the glory of heaven to become a man. In real human flesh, the Lord of eternity entered the realm of time. That eternal One would lie in his mother's arms, less than an hour old.

It is no wonder that Moses can say that, to God, a thousand years is like a watch in the night (90:4). A watch lasts for no more than a few hours – it may seem a long time when you are waiting for the dawn, but, on reflection, it is soon over. We often get impatient with the slow maturing of God's purposes, but you cannot hold an hourglass to the Creator of time.

Dust to dust
All this is contrasted with the brevity of human life.

Human beings are frail and fragile, feeble and fleeting. Echoing the words of Genesis 3, Moses reminds us that we are children of dust and feeble as frail (90:3).[3] Death is like sleep: irresistible and inevitable. Life is like the new grass that springs up in verdant beauty, but which then withers and disappears (90:5–6).

In words that sound like the tolling of a bell, he says,

All our days pass away under your wrath;
    we finish our years with a moan.
Our days may come to seventy years,
    or eighty, if our strength endures;
yet the best of them are but trouble and sorrow,
    for they quickly pass, and we fly away.
(Psalm 90:9–10)

We might think that Moses had a particularly jaded view of life – after all, almost everyone he had ever known had died before his eyes. That may be so, but, at the same time, his observations are also brutally realistic.

Speaking personally, I think that the darkest moment of Edrie's and my ordeal was when it dawned on me that she might not actually make it.

I had been with her since lunchtime and had travelled beside her in the ambulance as we crossed the city for an MRI scan. As I said earlier, trying to fit a heavily pregnant woman into the narrow confines of an MRI tube was quite a feat. We had had a good laugh about it on the way home – laughter really is quality medicine. But, as I had prepared to return home, the neurologist asked to see me. He had told me when he had first met me and discovered I was a pastor that he didn't believe in 'that kind of thing'. Now, he had to tell me that my wife was very ill and that I should be prepared for the fact that she might not live.

At such moments, every sensation seems to become either benumbed or intensified. I remember pulling at a piece of loose cotton on the cuff of my shirt. I recall the smell of disinfectant wafting in from the hospital ward. I looked down at the spines of the medical textbooks that were piled up on the neurologist's desk in apparent confusion as he told me the news. In what he must have thought was a concession to my faith, he said, 'We will do our best and hope for the best. Perhaps we can trust Mother Nature.' I remember thinking, 'I'd rather trust Father God.'

I don't know how I drove home – it's a bit of a blur really. And I don't know how I kept it from the kids. I felt cold and afraid and utterly alone. Edrie and I were both in our thirties and had never thought about death before. I remember praying, 'Lord, I don't mind if she is disabled, but please let me have her a little longer. The kids need their mum. I need my wife. Please don't take her.'

As a pastor, I have seen bereavement many times. I have sat with families at the bedside as lips have twitched for the final time and the last breath has left the body. I have seen people responding in a thousand different ways. I remember a woman from a small village in Wiltshire. She and her husband had been friends all their lives, having attended the same primary school together and grown up on adjacent farms. They had married in their teens and, for over sixty years, had not spent a single night apart. Now, he was gone. She told me, 'It feels like someone has pulled the flesh off my bones.'

Please don't tell me that Christians shouldn't grieve. The Bible tells us that we have hope, so we do not grieve like the world. However, nowhere does it ever suggest that the natural process of grieving is forbidden. When those we love depart, they are 'absent from the body'. We know that, as long as we live, we will never see that smile again, never feel the touch of that hand and never hear the timbre of that voice. Speaking personally, barely a day goes by when I do not think about my dad and long to see his smile and talk to him about the football results. He would be amazed that the Albion are doing so well and the Wolves so badly. I just want to share inconsequential flippancies with him. It's funny what you remember. My dad had been a grocer before he worked at Cadbury's. He had huge hands covered with small cuts, caused by preparing the side of bacon for the window. How I long to hold those hands again.

'It feels like someone has pulled the flesh off my bones.'

Of course we grieve. But those who have died in Christ are also 'present with the Lord'. That is our comfort and our solid assurance, which means that our grieving is not hopeless.

We live in a world that exists under the constant shadow of death. The eternal God created us in his image and placed eternity in our hearts. We know instinctively that there must be something more than this.

Justice and anger

Why should creatures created for eternity pass through the world so quickly? Did God make a mistake? Did he somehow miscalculate?

The Bible does not fudge these questions. Moses addresses them in the next section of Psalm 90. He recognizes God's hand at work: the death of the wilderness generation was the result of God's judgment. In verses 7–11, Moses uses a wide vocabulary of wrath as he describes God's response to their rebellion. They were 'consumed by his anger' and 'terrified by his indignation'. Their days are passed 'under his wrath'.

Perhaps we find these words disturbing. Isn't this just the Old Testament perspective, reminiscent of a little girl I once heard say, 'I don't like God in the Old Testament; I prefer him in the New Testament when he became a Christian'?

However, before we reject such statements, here are two important observations.

Firstly, God's anger is a biblical reality and must not be confused with intemperate human anger. God's anger is not capricious or arbitrary; it is never irascible or malicious or spiteful. God is often described as 'slow to anger and abundant in mercy'. The Jewish rabbis used to say that the angel of mercy flew on two wings, while the angel of wrath flew only on one wing. Unlike us, God is never quick and hasty, and his anger is never unpredictable, but it is always in response to wickedness. Wrath is God's righteous reaction to evil. It is his implacable hostility to sin and a sign of his refusal to condone it.

If we find it difficult to come to terms with this, then we only need to think of a world ruled by a God who was indifferent to injustice and did not care about evil. Would you really want to live in such a world? I wouldn't.

Secondly, we need to recognize that the anger of God is affirmed throughout the *whole* Bible. It is clear in the Old Testament, but, if anything, it is even more emphatic in the New Testament. Jesus and his apostles say a lot about the fate of those who die without Christ. Paul tells us that the glory of the gospel is that it rescues us from the wrath of God (Romans 1:16–18), and Hebrews reminds us that it is a dreadful thing to fall into the hands of the living God (10:31). In words which John Calvin described as the most terrifying in the Bible, John describes the day of judgment:

> Then the kings of the earth, the princes, the generals, the rich, the mighty, and everyone else, both slave and free, hid in caves and among the rocks of the mountains. They called to the mountains and the rocks, 'Fall on us and hide us from the face of him who sits on the throne and from the wrath of the Lamb! For the great day of their wrath has come, and who can withstand it?'
> (Revelation 6:15–17)

And of course, it is in the cross of Christ that the fullest displeasure of God against human sin was most clearly demonstrated. Here the eternally beloved Son of the Father took responsibility for the sins of all his people and bore the punishment that they deserved. The final and definitive proof of the wrath of God is the cross of Christ.

Spotlight on Genesis 3
Moses explains that the people perished in the wilderness because they had exhausted God's patience and incurred his righteous judgment. Half a million graves bear eloquent testimony to the reality of God's holy and emphatic response to human rebellion.

As we read these words, we cannot help but think about the account of the fall of humankind in Genesis 3.

Genesis 3 portrays historical realities. Christ and the apostles assume that Adam was an historical figure, and base their teaching on this foundation (Matthew 19:4–6; Mark 10:6–8; 1 Timothy 2:13).

However, Adam was more than a private individual. He represented the whole human race. His probation was the probation of the race, and his sin was the original sin that affected the race. God's judgment on Adam was his just judgment on all human beings.

When we wrestle with the problem of evil, this is one of the most important insights that the Bible gives us. Half a million graves in the wilderness, row upon row of white crosses in Flanders Fields and the tombs in the Glasgow necropolis testify to the universal facts of the human condition. Adam's sin brought the whole world under God's judgment.

Imagine a beautiful painting that has been slashed and ruined by a thoughtless vandal. But you can still see the beauty under the lacerations. This world is still a beautiful place, and echoes of infinity are all around us. At the same time, this is a damaged and cursed cosmos, a world under the just judgment of a holy God. You have never seen an unfallen tree or an unscathed sunset. And part of the character of this fallen world is that it is the realm of death. Indeed, death is a daily reality. The whole creation groans. Even in the midst of life, we are in death.

Numbering our days

Psalm 90 describes the tragedy of human suffering. But Moses does not leave us there. In the final section, he turns to God in prayer. Suffering can harden our hearts or it can soften them so that we seek God's grace and help. The psalm ends with a series of petitions.

In the first prayer, Moses asks for the wisdom which will offer clarity about the brief time we spend on this earth:

Teach us to number our days,
      that we may gain a heart of wisdom.
   (90:12)

God gives us little packets of time that we call days. Each one is a gift from God, and Moses asks that he might have wisdom so that no day is wasted. A year is made up of 365 packets of time. If you live to be seventy, you will experience somewhere in the region of 25,568 packets of time.

How do we number them rightly?

Firstly, we need to make the most of every one of them. They are so limited in number that we cannot afford to waste a moment. How much time do we fritter away? I remember thinking, after my talk with the neurologist: I want to make the most of every day God gives me with the most precious person in my universe. I don't want a day to go by without telling her that I love her and showing it in little acts of kindness. I remember giving each of my kids a particularly intense hug that night – gripping them for comfort, but also in the realization that time goes so quickly. One of my friends did a survey in his church, asking experienced parents what three pieces of advice they would give to new parents just beginning on the adventure of parenthood. There was a whole variety of responses, but, in every list, one piece of advice stood out: don't fritter away those early years with all their challenges and traumas; they are soon gone, and you will regret it. Long days, but short years.

Secondly, numbering our days forces us to think about eternity. We have eternity in our hearts and we need to set it before our eyes. We are creatures of eternity with an eternal destiny. A heart of wisdom recognizes that what we do in this life will echo on into eternity. Imagine a massive piece of paper. Draw a tiny dot with a pencil. Now draw a line from that dot. The line goes to the edge of the paper and then to the edge of the desk. It runs on and on, never stopping on this infinitely large canvas. The dot represents all the time we spend on this earth. The line represents eternity. You may live to be seventy or eighty, or ninety or even well over a hundred. Or you may die much younger. However long you live, compared to eternity, it is still only a tiny dot. The author of the book of Ecclesiastes captures this idea well:

> Now all has been heard;
>> here is the conclusion of the matter:
> fear God and keep his commandments,
>> for this is the duty of all mankind.
> For God will bring every deed into judgment,
>> including every hidden thing,
>> whether it is good or evil.
> (Ecclesiastes 12:13–14)

True wisdom

What does such wisdom look like? Moses describes it in the petitions that follow. Wisdom seeks God's mercy and forgiveness (90:13). It finds its satisfaction and joy in his unfailing love (90:14–15). It seeks to see and know his glory and splendour (90:16). All of these prayers are about relationship. In the midst of a transient world, Moses encourages us to find our focus in an intimate personal relationship with God.

This God is righteous and unremitting in his hatred of evil, but he is also amazingly gracious and compassionate. Moses asks that God would again smile on his servants and forgive their many sins (90:13). Seeing our sins in the light of his purity should not drive us to despair; it should drive us into the arms of the One whose nature is always to have mercy. God blots out our transgressions and separates our sins from us. The genuine cry for mercy is always met with a readiness to forgive, on the basis of Christ's sacrifice on the cross:

> When Satan tempts me to despair,
> And tells me of the guilt within,
> Upward I look, and see Him there

Who made an end to all my sin.
Because the sinless Saviour died,
My sinful soul is counted free;
For God, the Just, is satisfied
To look on Him and pardon me.[4]

Forgiveness brings us into the enjoyment of God himself. God satisfies us in the morning with his unfailing love (90:14), and the genuine joy which he inspires outweighs all the sorrows we may experience (90:15). It may come as a surprise, but, even in the middle of the book, we can know a deep healing joy. And this joy is not some superficial commodity based on temperament or circumstances. Even in the midst of fierce trials, we can have tears in our eyes and joy in our hearts. Joy is the spontaneous overflow of a heart that has experienced God's grace and knows that, in everything, God means us well. We've seen that suffering can drive us to God or it can drive us from him. When we choose to allow it to drive us into his arms, we discover great joy as we contemplate his glory (90:16).

A wasted life?

Finally, Moses prays that, in this transient and tragic world, God would establish the work of our hands (90:17).

It was Jim Elliot, the young American missionary martyr whose widow Elisabeth we met earlier, who challenged the church: 'That man is no fool who gives what he cannot keep to gain what he cannot lose.'[5]

Jim had been a missionary to the Auca Indians of Ecuador. On 8 January 1956, aged only twenty-eight, he and four other missionaries were slaughtered by those they had come to reach. Was Jim's short life wasted? No, God established the work of his hands. The tragedy became a defining moment in the history of evangelical missions. Hundreds of young people were inspired to take up missionary work, and thousands were moved to a deeper commitment to Christ.

After Jim's death, his wife Elisabeth also continued the work her husband had begun. In October 1958, she went to live with the Huaorani tribe along with her three-year-old daughter Valerie, and Rachel Saint, the wife of one of the other martyrs. Elisabeth continued working among these indigenous tribes until 1963.

I still like cemeteries. I don't think it's morbid. They remind me of the brevity of life and the vastness of eternity. They also remind me of a future beyond the middle of the book, when every cemetery will give up its dead and death will be no more:

> For the Lord himself will come down from heaven, with a loud command, with the voice of the archangel and with the trumpet call of God, and the dead in Christ will rise first. After that, we who are still alive and are left will be caught up together with them in the clouds to meet the Lord in the air. And so we will be with the Lord for ever. Therefore encourage one another with these words.
>
> (1 Thessalonians 4:16–18)

5. Knowing the One who knows us perfectly

The middle of the night

Why is it that things always look worse in the wee small hours of the morning?

During those weeks when Edrie was in hospital, I worked really hard to keep things together. Apart from the tears on the stairs (with which I opened this book), I'd like to think that I made a pretty good job of it. I was as upbeat as my personality allowed. I am a natural pessimist: while some people are temperamentally joyful, I am temperamentally miserable. But for the sake of Edrie and the kids, I did all I could to be positive and to expect the best.

But at night I went to pieces. After visiting the hospital, I would fall into bed dog tired. I would be asleep within minutes and would usually sleep deeply for a couple of hours. However, the moment I woke up, the horror of the situation would invade my mind and grip my imagination. It would usually be around two in the morning, and, for all my exhaustion, I knew that I would not be able to sleep again.

The worst night – and the best night – occurred after the meeting with the neurologist described in the last chapter. He had warned me quite early on that this was a serious condition. Now he was calling me into his office again and going even further:

'Your wife will probably not get better, but we will do everything we can to pull her through.'

'Pull her through' is a very ominous phrase.

As usual, my mind went into overdrive when I awoke that night around 2:15am. But somehow it seemed worse this time. There were so many thoughts running round my head that it would be impossible to articulate them all, but, in the end, they came down to one dominant fear: how can I work everything out for the best when I don't even know what tomorrow might bring? It sounds stupid when I say it: God does not expect us to know what tomorrow will bring – he promises to cover that base for us. But, like most of us, I wanted to work it out, to know and to understand. I guess I was reluctant to surrender control. On top of that, I felt neglected and forsaken by God. Did he care? Did he even know about our circumstances? It sometimes feels very lonely in the middle of the book. So, for almost two hours, I wrestled with every permutation and every possible scenario until I felt exhausted and spent and in utter despair.

Then God speaks

Then God spoke to me.

It wasn't an audible voice or a vision. But it was as powerful as if it had been. Into my mind came a verse from the Bible. Actually, it was only part of a verse: 'As for God, his way is perfect.' I knew it was in the Psalms, but I couldn't remember quite where. What was important was that a sovereign God has a perfect plan and that he would work out everything for his glory and our good. I was worried about tomorrow – I didn't need to be. All I had to do was to focus on the God who had plans for today and tomorrow and for all eternity. OK, I may not understand his ways – but I don't need to. What he calls me to do is to surrender all my concerns into his hands and trust him with my future.

It is difficult to describe, but immediately my heart was flooded with peace. It was 4:10 in the morning. Within a few moments, I found myself praising God for his goodness as I was filled with a new sense of confidence and joy. Shortly afterwards, I fell into the most restful sleep I had enjoyed in a long time.

When I awoke at 8:30am, I felt refreshed and still full of joy. I looked up the verse and found that it came from Psalm 18, a psalm written at the end of David's life as he looks back over all the way that God has led him (2 Samuel 22:1–51):

> As for God, his way is perfect:
>> the LORD's word is flawless;
>> he shields all those who take refuge in him.
> (Psalm 18:30)

David speaks of a perfect plan, a tested truth and a permanent protection. Mine was no 'content-free' existential experience. It was a genuine experience of the grace of God, conveyed to the heart by the objective reality of the truth about the character of God, mediated through his Word and applied by his Spirit.

There are no accidents that sneak in and take God by surprise.

God had an all-embracing plan that was eternal and comprehensive and invincible. More than that, I was part of that plan. In the dark watches of the night, I had felt forgotten. But I could now see that God knew everything about my circumstances: he knew all that Edrie and I were going through and he had plans for our future. There are no accidents that sneak in and take God by surprise. God does not tell us everything we want to know, but he does tell us all we need to know in order to trust him.

David's greatest psalm?

The great comfort of that night was remembering that God was not a distant and unconcerned deity. He was close by, and our circumstances were not hidden from his gentle gaze.

This is the great theme of Psalm 139, described as David's greatest psalm. Perhaps that is a subjective judgment, but it is certainly magnificent and sublime in its dimensions. There are hints that David was going through difficulties when he wrote it. He speaks of 'bloodthirsty' men who hate God and, by implication, hate his servants too (139:19–22). He is aware of anxious thoughts that have invaded his mind (139:23) and is concerned for his own purity and the integrity of his relationship with God (139:24). Against this background, he comforts himself with a reflection on the greatness of God's knowledge. In four stanzas, he worships the God whose knowledge is comprehensive, intimate and purposeful.

Perfect knowledge

David begins by describing God's comprehensive personal knowledge. He searches us with such a depth of understanding that nothing can be hidden from his gaze (verse 1). This verb evokes the image of searching for buried treasure.

When one of my sons was small, I would occasionally have to scold him. I noticed that, as I did so, he would screw up his eyes so that he could not see me. It dawned on me that, in his childish mind, if he couldn't see me, then maybe I couldn't see him! When we grow up, we put away such childish notions. Or do we? Often we conduct our lives as if the invisible God is also the uncomprehending God. We cannot see him, so does he really see us?

David reminds us that he does. In the next three verses, he reflects on how comprehensive God's knowledge actually is. Giving vivid and concrete examples, he tells us that God knows when we sit, when we rise, what we think, where we go, where we rest, where our way is leading, and, on top of all that, the words we will speak even before they are on our lips (2–4).

It strikes me that most of these things are quite banal and prosaic activities. Frankly, who counts the number of times that they sit down and stand up in an average day? Perhaps only the kinds of people who have wardrobes full of anoraks!

But that is the whole point. God knows the little insignificant and neglected details of our lives. What is more, he sees what no-one else can see. He 'perceive[s] my thoughts from afar' (139:2). I have seen my wife's brain – that is, I have seen the images taken from an MRI scan. But I cannot see her thoughts – the only access I have to those is what she chooses to reveal to me. But God knows the thoughts that no-one else sees or guesses or even imagines. Nothing can be hidden from his gaze. What is more, he knows them 'from afar'. He knows what you are thinking long before you think it. What will be in your mind in exactly one week from today or one year from today or ten years from today? No, you have no idea – but God does!

Omniscience

Theologians often refer to this as God's *omniscience*. It is God's absolute, comprehensive, all-encompassing, limitless knowledge.

I remember my first trip to Cambridge University Library. Sitting on the shelves were more books than I had ever seen in my life. (The library receives 80,000 new books every year.) It has been estimated that Cambridge University owns 12 million books in its 114 libraries, but the main university library is by far the biggest.[1] When I looked for commentaries on the prophecy of Isaiah, I found rows and rows of them in several languages. I thought I had died and gone to heaven. (There have to be books in heaven, don't there?) Imagine how long it would take you just to read all the books in Cambridge University Library. How long would it take not only to read them, but also to comprehend them and master their contents? Hundreds of lifetimes? Thousands of lifetimes? Yet all the accumulated knowledge in all the books in Cambridge University is less than a trillionth of a per cent of the knowledge that God has.

To David, this knowledge seems overwhelming – he feels hemmed in. God knows the hidden things of the past, and the secret things of the future. Like a friendly uncle or a kind mentor, God lays his hand on David's shoulder and tells him not to worry. He knows the best about him and the worst, and he loves him all the same (verse 5). He is a reliable guide and protector and provider. As David thinks about this, he is blown away. It is just too much to take in (verse 6).

What a source of immense comfort!

Personal knowledge

David then reflects on the *way* in which God knows us. It is not second hand, not like the Incident Room of the White House where the military chiefs of staff keep the President up to date with the most accurate intelligence that can be supplied by the most sophisticated spy satellites. God does not need to send angels down to earth to report back. God knows all things perfectly and instinctively, because all things happen as part of his plan. He is immediately present in every part of his universe. This is what theologians describe as his *omnipresence*. God has no size or spatial dimensions, but is present at every point in space with his whole being.

> *God knows the hidden things of the past, and the secret things of the future.*

David helps us to understand this by asking questions:

Where can I go from your Spirit?
> Where can I flee from your presence?
(139:7)

As you read this book, look around for a moment. Is a source of light visible? Can you see the colour of the walls, or the shadows playing on the ceiling? Is there someone nearby? What can you hear? What can you smell? We have a sense of the reality of everything in our immediate environment. But there is something more. Right now, you are in the immediate presence of God. The word 'presence' is a translation of the Hebrew word for 'face'. At this very moment, you are before the face of God. His eye is upon you.

And we are constantly before the face of the Lord. Every petty betrayal and every gross sin is seen by Christ. Every book we read, every DVD we watch, every website we visit, every unkind word we utter, God is at our shoulder.

To drive this home, David directs us to four spatial dimensions (8–10). From the highest heavens to the greatest depths, God is present. Up through the skies and out beyond the furthest star to the very throne room of God, you cannot escape him. In the ocean depths and even the grave itself, God is there. From the extreme east, where the sun rises, to the extreme west on the far side of the Mediterranean, God is present.

These are not the speculations of arid theology; they lead to wonder and comfort. Whatever his circumstances, David feels God's hand guiding and gripping him (139:10). We are safe because, in every corner of his universe, God is present not as an observer, but as a faithful friend. In the darkest night, he is close. The darkness is not dark to him.

Light in the darkness

I once visited a mining museum in Yorkshire. As part of the tour, we went underground and along the path the miners would have taken. At one point, our guide turned off the lights so we could experience what it must have been like for those trapped with their torches spent. It really is true that your other senses are heightened. I could hear the steady drip of water in the cave, feel the slight breath of wind and see the tiny glow of light from people's wristwatches. In fact, the profound darkness was quite unnerving. How terrifying it must have been for the men caught down there, listening anxiously for any sound that might inform them that they were not forgotten, that help was on its way.

In the dark watches of the night, I had felt bereft and forsaken by God. But, all the time, he was close by.

Dutch sisters Betsie and Corrie ten Boom were arrested by the Nazis for protecting Jewish people fleeing from the Holocaust. The sisters were thrown into Ravensbrück Concentration Camp. Corrie survived, but Betsie didn't. However, they both testified to the presence of God with them in one of the darkest places on earth. Before her death, Betsie told her sister that, if Corrie survived, she must tell others about the faithfulness of God: 'There is no pit so deep, that God's love is not deeper still . . . In darkness God's truth shines most clear.'[2]

Permanent knowledge

The next part of the psalm is one of the most breath-taking passages in the Bible (139:13–18). David reminds us that God has always known us. From the first flutter of life to the last beat of our heart, we are on his mind.

David has been speaking about the dark and mysterious places of this earth, and surely one of the most mysterious of all dark and secret places is the womb in which we first experienced life. Yet God was there, knitting us together and weaving our innermost being like a master craftsman. In days before embryology and ultrasound scans, David tells us that the Creator of supernovas and black holes and dark matter is concerned with the colour of your eyes and the shape of your ears and the length of your toes.

Modern prenatal science explores the role of chromosomes and cell division, but David assures us that before and behind all these natural processes is the personal hand of a gracious deity. There is a friend behind the phenomena. With care and precision and attention to detail, God has formed us to be exactly what he wants us to be. From a single fertilized cell comes a Beethoven or an Einstein or you.

No wonder David says,

> I praise you because I am fearfully and wonderfully made;
>> your works are wonderful,
>> I know that full well.
>
> (139:14)

In the last twenty years, I have met many neurologists. They are very skilful people but, in the end, they will readily admit that there are limits to their understanding of the workings of the human brain. We like to think that we are dwellers in the realms of explanation. But our knowledge is in fact severely limited.

Just a few years ago, we had another disappointing hospital appointment. Most of us have confidence in the medical profession and great respect for its achievements, and rightly so. But serious illness forces us to recognize its limitations. As we drove home, I remember Edrie, the natural optimist in our relationship, being particularly downcast. We got home and she lay in my arms and we just poured out our souls to God. She whispered in my ear, 'Even if the doctors don't know what is going on, there is Someone who does.'

Some sources tell us that the average adult human body is made up of 50 million million (50 trillion) cells.[3] Others put the figure closer to 10 trillion. But God knows every one of them. The perfect God knew you before you were born – indeed the Bible tells us that we were in his mind in eternity. He knew you when you were a single fertilized cell. He knew you as that cell divided and multiplied again and again. Nothing was hidden from his tender and fatherly gaze.

The end of days

If God knows the beginning of our lives, then he also knows the end:

All the days ordained for me were written in your book
before one of them came to be.
(139:16)

We cannot live one day longer than God has ordained or die one day before he permits. We can rest in the perfection of God's purposes and the wisdom of his ways.

David Watson was an Anglican clergyman, an early Charismatic and one of the finest preachers and evangelists I have ever heard. When he was diagnosed with cancer, he wrote a moving book that described his struggle with that atrocious disease. It was called *Fear No Evil*,[4] and it has been a blessing to many people in similar circumstances down through the years. David was convinced that God was able to heal him if he wanted to. Instead, however, God chose to take him home to heaven.

I attended a Bible study a few weeks after news of David's death had broken. One of the guys taking part in the discussion was quite adamant:

'David Watson should not have died. It was not God's will. David's faith must have slipped, and then the devil killed him.'

We have met that kind of thinking before. Just work through the implications for a moment. God has this wonderful plan for our lives in which every one of us lives to a ripe old age. But the plan can be derailed if somehow our faith slips and a demonic hit man takes us out. Presumably, we are welcomed into heaven by a frustrated but basically impotent deity.

The idea is preposterous! We cannot live a day longer than he has ordained, but neither can we die a day before he has determined. That is both biblically accurate and profoundly comforting. In our most painful moments, this fact has brought Edrie and me deep consolation and reassurance.

David closes the stanza with another exclamation of wonder and praise:

How precious to me are your thoughts, God!
  How vast is the sum of them!
Were I to count them,
  they would outnumber the grains of sand –
  when I awake, I am still with you.
(Psalm 139:17–18)

You are on God's mind. He is thinking about you.

The sting in the tail

We might be tempted to leave the psalm there, but David won't let us. In the final stanza, he turns to God in prayer. How can such a powerful God allow such opposition to his purposes? How bizarre: humans are utterly dependent on God from the first moment of life to the end of our days. Yet we shake our fists in the face of our Creator. Such crass rebellion is both foolish and evil. He describes such rebels as wicked and bloodthirsty men. They speak of God with evil intent and misuse his name.

In words that might offend our sentiments, David confesses,

Do I not hate those who hate you, LORD,
  and abhor those who are in rebellion against you?
I have nothing but hatred for them;
  I count them my enemies.
(139:21–22)

At first sight, this looks very different from the New Testament command to turn the other cheek. But think again. David is not seeking revenge for personal slights against himself; he is passionate about God's glory. What is more, he is not taking matters into his own hands, but placing them into God's hands.

When the world seems enigmatic and evil people seem to flourish, what are we to do? We must always oppose evil and be on the side of the truth. But in the final analysis, we can hand over our concerns to God and leave them with him. His righteousness is impeccable and his justice is perfect. One day he will certainly right all wrongs.

In the end, David does not just lash out with anger at those who hate God. He is conscious of the sin that lingers in his own heart and asks God to detect it and root it out (139:23–24).

Immensity of being . . . intensity of love

All this is pretty heady stuff. This is a psalm about the immensity of God's being, about the all-knowing, all-filling, all-seeing, all-present, all-powerful and all-holy God. The twenty-four verses are dominated by this God. It is no wonder that David says,

> Such knowledge is too wonderful for me,
>> too lofty for me to attain.
> (139:6)

However, the psalm also reminds us of the intensity of his love. It is not just sublime theology; it is also personal testimony. From the very beginning, David is speaking about an intimate personal relationship. Count the number of times he uses the personal pronouns 'I' or 'me' or 'my'.

God is reachable and knowable and available and real.

Of course, the psalm is about God's knowledge of all things – from the far-flung galaxies to the depths of the atom. But David's emphasis is on God's personal knowledge of his life and circumstances. When we feel forgotten and deserted, we need to remember that God knows us, and, even in the darkest night, he is making his plans for us. God is reachable and knowable and available and real.

And he invites us into a relationship with himself. The One who knows us is also the One who wants to be known by us. During that dark and wonderful night so many years ago, I felt the reality of God's presence as he whispered in my ear:

'Trust me – my way is perfect.'

6. Perfect way, perfect purposes

Cricket dreams

I couldn't wait to get to the hospital to tell Edrie about my night-time epiphany. The joy of resting in the fact that God's way was perfect made me feel like a new man.

It was a warm Saturday in late June. Edrie's radiant smile greeted me when I walked into the ward. She had been moved from Neurology to Maternity, since the birth was imminent.

Edrie had had a bad night, but was as brave as ever. I told her I had something I wanted to tell her and asked the ward sister if I could take my wife for a walk in the grounds. The sister was a little anxious but, in the end, agreed that I could have Edrie for an hour. So I pushed the wheelchair out of the hospital and across to a field where a game of cricket was in progress. I helped Edrie from the wheelchair onto a bench, and we watched the match for a while.

There is something immensely soothing about a Saturday-afternoon cricket match on a warm day at the height of English summer. For a little while, we just sat in each other's arms and told each other things that I am certainly not going to share with my readers!

Then I began to describe the previous night and the comfort it had brought me. I opened my Bible, and we read part of Psalm 18 together. I showed her what God had showed me from the psalm.

I remember saying, 'What I have come to see is that we have to hand things over to the Lord. We like to be in control – we don't like to be in the hands of someone else, because it makes us feel vulnerable. But that is where God wants us to be. His way is perfect, and we have to trust that he knows what he is doing.'

Worry has an active imagination

Edrie saw it straight away. We had been worried about her health problems, worried about the baby she was carrying, worried about our other kids, worried about how I would continue in ministry – or even if I would be able to remain a pastor. Most of all, we were anxious about living in a scary world that was so different from the world we had grown used to.

We worry because we have active imaginations. We have active imaginations because we have been made in the image of a Creator who has an infinite imagination. He could imagine kangaroos and orchids and black holes and Mount Everest, and then speak them into existence. Imagination is a good thing. But when we poor frail creatures allow our imaginations to go into overdrive, we are apt to become unduly anxious and fearful.

Yet we know that the future is uncharted. When all is going well, you can be optimistic and upbeat – indeed, it can be exciting to look across an ocean of possibilities. But when you are in the middle of a storm and cannot see beyond the shadow of the next wave that is about to upend your pathetic little boat, it suddenly becomes terrifying. We were on very choppy seas. We had been buoyant about the future. Now everything was unpredictable and frightening and unknown.

What was so helpful about the words from Psalm 18 was that they encouraged us to put everything into God's hands and believe that his plans for us could not be frustrated. Indeed, we had to see that the painful experiences of life were actually part of the plan. God wanted to use our suffering to bless us and others too.

As we talked, it began to dawn on us that God was fitting us for a new stage of ministry. That afternoon, we came to see that he intended to use our miseries to minister his mercy to others.

The hour was almost gone. With the sound of the leather on willow in the background, I knelt on the ground next to the bench and we both talked to God. It went something like this:

> Lord, we don't know why you have sent this and we would be really glad if you would take it away. But we trust you and we believe that your way is perfect. Help us to trust you more. And help us to see this as part of your plan for our lives. Lord, we want to serve you and be channels of blessing to others. Please help us not to get bitter; help us to be available. Help us to use what you have sent us to help others as they struggle with the mysteries of your dark providences. Please give us the grace we need. Amen.

I don't know what other people thought as they saw a heavily pregnant woman in a dressing-gown sitting on a bench with a man on his knees at her feet looking up into heaven imploringly. Perhaps they thought I was belatedly proposing marriage! I didn't care a hoot. I was beginning to imagine the future, with God using even our most painful experiences to bless both us and others. As the umpire signalled a boundary, we returned to the ward.

When I eventually got home, I tried to explain a little of this to the kids. I'm not sure how much of it they took in. But for Edrie and me, it had been a decisive moment. We were turning over our future to God and asking him to use our experiences. We certainly didn't like what was happening to us, but we were available. We didn't want to waste what God was pouring into our lives.

Crushed beyond measure

The concept of being crushed beyond measure is a common theme in the Bible. When we are in pain, where do we turn? To those who have been right where we are. Job passed through the most excruciating agony imaginable. Did he think that, thousands of years later, people would be turning for comfort to the book that describes his experiences? Probably not. The same is true of the laments in the Psalms or the grief-gripped cries of Jeremiah or the sober musings of Ecclesiastes.

In the New Testament, we find comfort and help from the words of the apostle Paul, words wrung from a bruised and battered heart. We sometimes think of Paul as the supreme theologian of the early church, its great missionary strategist and its evangelist par excellence. Perhaps we picture him as a man who had everything worked out, the ultimate 'cool communicator'.

Then we read words like these:

> We do not want you to be uninformed, brothers and sisters, about the troubles we experienced in the province of Asia. We were under great pressure, far beyond our ability to endure, so that we despaired of life itself. Indeed, we felt we had received the sentence of death . . .
> (2 Corinthians 1:8–9)

There's nothing 'cool' about that! Paul's words show the intensity of his suffering. He is 'under great pressure', crushed under a great weight. He feels as if all his resources of courage and strength are spent. Like a prisoner on death row, he even '[feels] the sentence of death'.

He experienced much distress and hardship because of his faithfulness to Christ. And he ministered to others out of these experiences. Indeed, he was convinced that the purpose of suffering was to fit him for ministry. His ministry flowed out of his hardships. He seems to suggest that a personal familiarity with pain is an essential prerequisite for sensitive pastoral care.

It goes with the territory

The words 'crushed beyond measure' (also translated as 'utterly burdened beyond our strength') are taken from the first chapter of Paul's second letter to the Corinthians.

The Corinthians were troubled by a new breed of teachers who had invaded the church. Paul calls them 'super apostles'. He is being sarcastic – frankly, they are not really apostles at all. The essence of their message is that real servants of God would be more remarkable than Paul, who is not particularly impressive at all. What is more, real apostles would not suffer as Paul has suffered. To put it bluntly, Paul is a bit of an embarrassment.

Paul doesn't duck the issue. Indeed, he ripostes by cataloguing the sufferings he has endured for the sake of the gospel. He has been imprisoned and endangered, flogged and beaten, stoned and shipwrecked. He was in constant danger and felt crushed under the daily pressure of caring for the churches (2 Corinthians 11:21–29).

He goes even further. Suffering is the mark of a true apostle. Ordeals and distresses and troubles and hardships go with the territory. This is the cost and inevitable context of all true ministry. Paul's sufferings are the result of being a servant of a crucified Saviour. They are not a mark of shame, but a badge of honour.

Overflowing life

So what is the purpose of such suffering? In 2 Corinthians 1:5–6, Paul describes a clear sequence.

Step one: The sufferings of Christ flow over into our lives. We share abundantly. Christ suffered because he had come to obey his Father's will. If we are servants of Christ, we should expect to share his suffering. We follow a crucified Saviour and therefore should expect to live crucified lives. Notice that Paul does not envisage a little trickle of suffering – he is thinking of a flood swelling up and flowing over from Christ to us.

Step two: In the midst of these trials, God's comfort also flows over into our lives through Christ. God comforted his Son in the ordeal he passed through, and this comfort now overflows to us. We are united to Christ and therefore experience all the comforts and blessings that he experienced. Notice again that we are not thinking of a trickle but a flood.

Step three: This is the climax of the sequence. Our lives are like a goblet. First suffering flows in and then comfort flows in. Then, out from our lives flow the comforts that just flowed in. So our lives become a source of blessing and help to those around us. When we first experience the suffering that faithfulness to Christ brings, we may well be troubled and perplexed. But look at the outcome, says Paul. Personally, you will experience the wonderful comfort of God in your own life. But, more than that, you will find yourself equipped and enabled to be a blessing to others. Through you, they find the grace to endure.

Ministry of encouragement

Paul then drives this home:

> If we are distressed, it is for your comfort and salvation; if
> we are comforted, it is for your comfort, which produces
> in you patient endurance of the same sufferings we suffer.
> And our hope for you is firm, because we know that just as
> you share in our sufferings, so also you share in our comfort.
> (2 Corinthians 1:6–7)

The key word in this passage is the word 'comfort'. In the original, it can mean 'to exhort' or 'to encourage' or 'to comfort' or 'to console'. It suggests drawing alongside someone in order to help them to endure, even when they are feeling like giving up. It is pointing someone to where they can find the courage and confidence to persevere.

Anyone engaged in pastoral ministry should have a 'thick skin but a tender heart'.

Suffering forges us, making our hearts tender and gentle and sympathetic. My first pastor was a man called Les Coley. He was a great preacher and a wise friend. When I told him of my call into the ministry, he said, 'Anyone engaged in pastoral ministry should have a thick skin but a tender heart.' What gives you a tender heart? Suffering that softens and makes it a vehicle through which God can minister his mercy.

That is why Christ is the perfect comforter of his people: 'Because he himself suffered when he was tempted, he is able to help those who are being tempted' (Hebrews 2:18).

Do you see the principle? God sends suffering in order to fit us for service.

John Bunyan

Generations of Christians have been blessed and inspired by *The Pilgrim's Progress*. It was written while John Bunyan was incarcerated in Bedford jail for refusing to stop preaching. George Whitefield, the eighteenth-century evangelist, said of it:

It smells of the prison . . . and ministers never write or preach so well as when under the cross: the Spirit of Christ and glory then rests upon them.[1]

The Pilgrim's Progress has been translated into 200 languages and has never been out of print. It has been such a blessing because it combines a wonderfully fertile imagination with great biblical truths and a penetrating insight into the human heart.

What gave John Bunyan such a tender and perceptive grasp of the human condition? What equipped him? It was the fact that his heart had been bruised and broken and then remade by God's grace.

Bunyan was imprisoned for a total of twelve years. He and his wife Elizabeth had four children. Mary, the oldest, had been born blind. The years during which he languished in Bedford jail were tough on the whole family. But it was the impact on Mary that Bunyan felt most keenly. In his spiritual biography *Grace Abounding to the Chief of Sinners*, he wrote:

> The parting with my wife and poor children hath often
> been to me in this place as a pulling of the flesh from the
> bones . . . especially my poor blind child, who lay nearer my
> heart than all I had besides; O the thoughts of the hardship
> my blind one might go under, would break my heart to
> pieces.[2]

Like Paul, John Bunyan felt crushed and almost overwhelmed.

But it was right there in prison that God was forging an instrument he could use. There he met with Bunyan and spoke to his heart in the darkest hours of his life. The Bible became his most precious possession:

> I have never had in my life so great an inlet into the word of
> God as now. Those scriptures that I saw nothing in before were
> made in this place and state to shine upon me; Jesus Christ also
> was never more real and apparent than now. Here I have seen
> him and felt him indeed . . .[3]

God poured affliction into his life and then he poured it out in blessing. And that blessing has flowed out into the lives of countless men and women ever since.

Picture Bunyan as he grasps his fragile little daughter in his arms. She weeps. He weeps. He kisses her affectionately, and she buries her face in his chest. Then, Elizabeth tenderly takes her from his grasp and out through the door of the cell. The heavy door clangs shut. Bunyan feels utterly bereft and totally alone. He would do almost anything to avoid this parting. In fact, all he has to do is agree to stop preaching the gospel and he will be a free man. But that is the one thing he cannot do. He has a higher allegiance. He follows a crucified Saviour. Suffering goes with the territory. And so he sits on the ground and pours out his heart to God. And, as he does so, the Lord draws near as never before and, through the words of Scripture, pours comfort into his heart. He picks up his pen and begins to write . . .

Did Bunyan know that his suffering was purposeful? Did he know that it would result in the most famous Christian book next to the Bible? Did he know that tens of thousands of people would be encouraged and consoled and comforted by his book? Of course not! But without the pain and the heartache of those years, there would have been no copies of *The Pilgrim's Progress*.

In a lesser way, all our suffering is like that: designed to help others. And everyone you meet needs it.

Show me Jesus

The first series of sermons that I ever preached as young pastor was on the letter of James. I chose James because it was so practical and challenging. In those days, I subscribed to a fairly militant model of preaching. The job of the preacher was to be combative – exposing all sin and rooting out all offences – a kind of council for the prosecution. The mark of a good sermon was that it left the congregation deeply disturbed and profoundly uncomfortable. The greater the wriggle and squirm, the more successful it had been! And so, I preached with the naïve gusto and aggressive vigour of a shepherd who thought that the best way to tend his flock was by thrashing them.

After six months, I asked my elders how they thought I was doing. They were very kind. But Roland, a gentle and very godly soul, said, 'I hope you don't mind me saying this, but sometimes I come to church feeling fairly low and after your sermon, I go away feeling even worse. Sometimes, it would be good if you would just show us Jesus and encourage us.'

I am so grateful to God for that advice. Yes, we must confront sin and help people to battle with evil. Preaching has been compared to stamping on the devil's head. But our task as preachers is bigger than that. We are also to comfort the weak and bind up their wounds. Many Christians come to church feeling pretty bruised and battered already. We feel as if we have failed in our discipleship. It's not that we are complacent about our faith – it's just that we have come from a tough battle and still bear the scars. Sometimes, we do need to hear the clear warnings of Scripture, but these are always designed to bring us to trust Jesus more. What we need is a vision of the loveliness of Jesus, which will inspire and sustain us and just keep us going.

Roland's advice has stayed with me over the years. I tried to put it into practice before Edrie became unwell. But since Edrie's illness, it has been a watchword for my ministry. I like to think that suffering has made me a better pastor and a more sympathetic preacher and more effective evangelist. I look out on a congregation knowing that the best thing I can do for them is to make much of Jesus and speak well of him. He has been the great comfort in my darkest days – I know he can be the same for them.

> *'Three things make a preacher: prayer, meditation and suffering.'*

Martin Luther once asked, 'What makes a preacher?' He answered his own question: 'Three things make a preacher: prayer, meditation and suffering.'

He was right.

New directions in ministry

When Edrie and I sat in the sunshine outside the hospital on that warm June day so many years ago and prayed together, we were acknowledging the same truth. We were asking that we might humbly and submissively align our wills with God's, and not resist what he might send. We were expressing a desire to be available at any cost.

As I've said, one of the many fears we shared was that Edrie's illness might spell the end of our ministry together. How could I pastor a church when I had to nurse my wife and care for my children? I had even considered the possibility that I might have preached my last sermon. Now we prayed that our new insight might mark the beginning of a new and even more productive ministry.

Did God answer our prayers? Overwhelmingly yes, in more ways than we could possibly have imagined.

I have remained in ministry, and there have been countless moments when our experiences have formed the context of pastoral care or sermon application. I cannot remember how many times we have been with people in the darkest moments of their lives, and, as they have opened their hearts to us, there has been a moment's pause and they have said, 'Of course, you know all about this – you have been there, haven't you?' We have.

God has crushed us so that we can minister out of our pain. We have been able to 'rejoice with those who rejoice; mourn with those who mourn' (Romans 12:15).

People love Edrie. They love her compassion and her bravery and her sense of humour. They trust her promises to pray. I sometimes wake up in the middle of the night to find her in prayer – sleep has eluded her, and so she is carrying people to the Lord Jesus and laying them at his feet. She often joins me when we are counselling individuals. She sits quietly, and I do most of the talking. People listen to what I am saying, and it seems to help. And then, just before we close, Edrie adds a short word which goes to the heart of the problem. And that's what they remember!

The Lord is good

Edrie and I are currently visiting a young mum in our congregation. She is a beautiful young woman with a delightful family and she is dying of cancer. We have visited before, and now the end is not far off. When we visit, we open the Bible and read Psalm 100 together. We concentrate on the last verse:

> The LORD is good and his mercy endures for ever;
> his faithfulness continues through all generations.

We talk and pray and weep together. Then, Edrie begins to describe her experiences of God's goodness during these years: 'You know, there have been so many times when I just haven't understood what God was doing; times when I was frustrated and afraid and it all seemed too much. But, during all of it, I have found that God stayed close, and I can tell you that you can trust his goodness.' This carries credibility because it's not bland cheerfulness, but truth purchased through the agony of personal experience.

We rise to leave, and this woman's four children flood into the room. Her oldest daughter stands protectively at the head of her mum's bed. The two little boys sit beside the bed and begin to play with their toys. The smallest child, a little girl of two or three, just crawls into her mum's arms and settles down in her

warm and safe embrace. The scene is poignant beyond imagination, and Edrie and I have to work hard to hide our tears from
the kids. Then the mother calls me back and, with a smile that
I will never forget, she whispers in my ear, 'The Lord is so good,
isn't he? Please go on telling people that the Lord is good.'

In some small way, the comfort we have received has in turn
been a comfort in this heart-breaking situation.

In fact, the 'cricket dreams' of that lazy June afternoon of so
many years ago have been realized over and over again. Our
prayer has been answered a thousand times.

7. Developing the family likeness

Waiting

The moment finally arrived for Edrie to give birth.

She had spent six weeks in Neurology. We had certainly had our moments there. One day, the consultant had done his rounds accompanied by a group of aspiring medical students. Edrie was sitting up in bed with her knees raised. The consultant asked the first student to make any observations that he thought might be relevant. He looked at the charts, felt her pulse, conducted a few standard neurological tests and asked her some questions. Then, he confidently made some remarks about her condition. The consultant asked if there was anything else that struck him as relevant.

'I don't think so,' he replied.

'Mrs Mallard, will you please put your knees down.'

When she did so, it became obvious that the confident young clinician had missed the very small detail that his patient was eight months pregnant. Such fun!

But now we were in Maternity to wait for the birth.

Amid all our anxieties, it had been difficult to get excited, but the change of scenery brought with it a change of mood.

We began to talk about the baby – we didn't know whether it was a boy or a girl. We already had Caleb and Amos and Keziah – it would be great to have another little girl so that we had two of each. We talked about names. We prayed together and asked God to keep the baby well. We were anxious about whether he or she might have been affected by Edrie's condition. And Edrie prayed that, when the time came for her to return home, she would be able to walk into our house carrying the baby.

One afternoon, I arrived to find Edrie quite pensive.

'Will you promise me something?' she asked. 'If there has to be a choice between me and our baby, will you promise that you will choose to let our baby live?'

I avoided answering. I couldn't face the possibility of such a choice.

Clever Daddy

The first two deliveries, of our two boys, had been straight-forward, and Edrie had loved the experience. Then the birth of Keziah had been incredibly traumatic. That time, Edrie had been in hospital for two months with *placenta previa*. In the end, she had had to have an emergency C-section. With the alarms going off and the nurses rushing her along the corridor to the operating theatre, it was indeed a harrowing experience. I had paced up and down in the waiting room until the midwife had come in holding a little bundle of life.

'Your wife is fine, and you can see her in a few minutes. Is it two sons you have already, Mr Mallard? Yes? Well, who's been a clever daddy then!'

She handed our first little girl to me. Keziah was gorgeous, and I fell instantly in love. Edrie was bruised and battered but anxious to meet our daughter. When I returned the next day, she was much recovered and beginning to feed Kez. I bought a bright pink jumper in honour of the occasion when I introduced my sons to their new sister.

Edrie recovered quickly after that, but was adamant that she would never have another Caesarean.

A fraught time

Now, armed with this conviction, we talked to the midwives as Edrie prepared for her fourth baby. She was very weak and fragile, but she was determined that, if at all possible, she would give birth naturally. On reflection, it might have been better to consider other options, but Edrie was keen that, after so many weeks of trauma, the birth itself should be as normal as possible.

Edrie went into labour, and we headed down to the delivery suite. She was exceedingly brave and resolute. She worked so hard through hours of painful labour. I encouraged her, even though I was becoming increasingly fearful. In the end, her illness took its toll. After ten hours of pushing, her stamina was gone, she was spent, and the birth was still some way off. The midwife and attendant physician were becoming more and more anxious. Faced with a growing crisis, they decided that Edrie needed an emergency Caesarean. History was repeating itself.

This time, however, things were even more fraught, and they actually allowed me into the operating theatre. Standing at one end of the table, I held Edrie's hand while, at the other, they did all that was necessary to deliver the baby. An epidural meant that there was no pain, but Edrie was *in extremis*. Her small reserves of energy were spent, and the birth was traumatic.

However, Emmaus Louisa Edrie Mallard was born on 1 July 1992 at 9:02pm, and she was perfectly healthy. And Edrie had survived.

I stayed as long as I could and then drove home, made the obligatory phone calls and fell into bed. I woke up next morning, and rang the hospital. Edrie had had a quiet night, and they told me that I should come as soon as I could. Her life was not in danger, but she needed me to be there.

The drive to the hospital took forty minutes. It gave me time to reflect. Our lives had now changed forever. We had a new baby who appeared to be fit and healthy. That was great. But Edrie would never be the same again. Lots of people had assured me that, once the baby was born, Edrie would get better. But I was not convinced. Neither was her neurologist. He had not yet given her illness a name, but the dreaded words 'multiple sclerosis' had been bandied about, as mentioned earlier in this book. I had looked it up and didn't like what I found. As I drove to the hospital that morning, I found myself crying out to God. I still held on to the promise that God's plan was perfect, but I wanted him to show me *why* he was sending this test.

God must love me very much

As I drove, I reflected on a pastoral visit I had made a couple of years earlier. I had just conducted a funeral for an elderly member of the congregation. He had been married for many years, and his widow had been broken-hearted but brave. Less than a month after the funeral, I got a phone call from her, telling me that her son had been killed in an accident.

Two bereavements in such a short period of time, one of them totally unexpected, is a horrendous ordeal. I drove across town to her house, all the while asking God to help me to know what to say.

She answered the door with tears streaked across her face. Before I could utter a word, she said, 'Thank you so much for coming, pastor. I'm glad you are here. The Lord must love me very much to let me pass through this test. I suppose it's the only way he can make me like Jesus.'

As I drove to the hospital that morning, her words came back to me. Did I believe that God was still in control? Did I believe that this was not evidence of God's neglect, but of his loving care? Most of all, did I believe that one of the principal reasons behind all that we were experiencing was to make us like Jesus?

Creating character

When God saves us, it is his purpose to transform us. The moment that we believe, God sets us aside to belong to him. He adopts us as his sons and daughters. Then he spends the rest of our lives changing us so that we begin to display the family likeness.

Jesus Christ is the eternal Son of God, and he perfectly reflects and demonstrates God's character. What is God like? He is exactly like Jesus. In his life and his ministry, in his teaching and his acts of mercy, in his death and resurrection, he reveals the Father. He is the perfect and final standard of holiness.

God is at work in our lives, making us like Jesus, a continuous process that will never be completed in this life. One day, when Jesus returns, we will see him as he is and will instantly be transformed into his likeness (1 John 3:2). Only then will the process of sanctification be complete.

In the meantime, God is at work in the long, laborious process of creating character. God demands our full cooperation; we are to 'work out [our] salvation with fear and trembling' (Philippians 2:12). Like a soldier in a battle or an athlete in a race or a boxer in the ring, we are to work hard at Christian discipleship. We are to 'put to death' our old desires and passions, and feed our new longings and spiritual cravings.

For his part, God is committed to us and determined to change us to become more like Jesus. For this, he uses a number of tools. And suffering is probably the sharpest tool in his box. Trials are necessary in the creation of character.

Into the furnace

The Bible uses a number of images to describe the way in which God shapes our lives through suffering.

One is like the purification of silver in a furnace. The psalmist describes it in this way:

> For you, God, tested us;
>> you refined us like silver.
> You brought us into prison
>> and laid burdens on our backs.
> You let people ride over our heads;
>> we went through fire and water,
>> but you brought us to a place of abundance.
> (Psalm 66:10–12)

Tests are not accidental, but part of God's deliberate plan. At the time, they are severe and painful. Just look at the metaphors. However, trials are limited: we will one day come into a place of abundance. Trials are also purposeful.

Imagine that, one day, I am walking along the road and accidentally kick a stone. I pick it up and find that it is just a lump of rock. It is of no value, so I throw it away. But imagine that, as I turn the rock in my hand, I discover that there is a vein of silver running through the heart of it. What do I do? I take it home and crush it. When it is ground into powder, I put it into the hottest furnace I can find. I heat it until all the dross is consumed. Then I remove the dross and am left with pure silver.

If the lump of rock could speak, what would it say?

'Why are you crushing me? Why have you placed me in this painful place?'

And the answer?

'It is because I have seen that you have value. You are precious to me, because I can see the silver in the midst of the dross.'

We assume that, in our trials, God has forgotten us or that they prove that we are of no value to him. Precisely the opposite is true. God tests us because we are precious and he wants to remove the dross and prove the reality of our faith. The fire of the furnace is proof of intentional grace and deliberate mercy.

In the hands of the vinedresser

A second image is that of pruning a vine: 'I am the true vine, and my Father is the gardener. He cuts off every branch in me that bears no fruit, while every branch that does bear fruit he prunes so that it will be even more fruitful' (John 15:1–2).

Vines were a common sight in Israel. Only expert vinedressers were allowed anywhere near them. One of the most demanding parts of the job was to discern the amount of foliage to cut away in order to produce optimum fruit. Sometimes, the vinedresser cut away unhealthy branches, sometimes healthy branches. The purpose was always that there would be more fruit.

God prunes 'every branch'. This is a universal Christian experience. It is often the adverse circumstances of life that form the scalpel in the hands of the divine Vinedresser. God may cut away unhealthy and diseased branches from our lives. But, on other occasions, God may remove good and healthy and potentially fruitful branches. He does this so that we may be even more fruitful. We understand it when suffering is used to remove sinful desires and passions. But what about those times when God takes away good and healthy things? That is harder to bear. However, we still have to believe that the expert Vinedresser does know what he is doing.

God disciplines his children

A third image is that of parental care and discipline. In the circumstances described at the beginning of this chapter, this seems the most appropriate image to dwell on. For this, we will turn to the book of Hebrews, the context to which the woman with the double bereavement was alluding:

The Lord must love me very much to let me pass through this
test. I suppose it's the only way he can make me like Jesus.

Hebrews is addressed to a group of Jewish Christians facing
persecution because of their allegiance to Jesus. They are being
tempted to give up and return to Judaism. The author tells them
that it may be difficult going on, but it is impossible to go back.

The author urges his readers to step back from their current
circumstances and see that the suffering they are experiencing is
part of God's purpose.

> Therefore, since we are surrounded by such a great cloud of
> witnesses, let us throw off everything that hinders and the sin
> that so easily entangles. And let us run with perseverance the
> race marked out for us, fixing our eyes on Jesus, the pioneer
> and perfecter of faith. For the joy that was set before him he
> endured the cross, scorning its shame, and sat down at the right
> hand of the throne of God. Consider him who endured such
> opposition from sinners, so that you will not grow weary and
> lose heart.
> (Hebrews 12:1–3)

He starts by comparing life to a gruelling race. They may feel
like giving up, but they have to suck it up and keep going. They
can only do this as they keep their eyes on Jesus. In this spiritual
marathon, he is the pacemaker who runs ahead to lead the way
and inspire renewed exertion. They can be confident, because
he finishes what he starts.

As we struggle with trials, we are to remember that Christ
is for us. He was born for us; he lived for us; he died for us; he
rose for us; he reigns for us; he prays for us; he is coming again
for us. We are to consider carefully all that he endured for us. As
he went to the cross, he set us an example of faithful endurance,
looking beyond the agonies of the race to the reward promised
to all who compete successfully.

The author then changes direction and uses the analogy of faithful fatherhood to help them understand their suffering:

In your struggle against sin, you have not yet resisted to the point of shedding your blood. And have you completely forgotten this word of encouragement that addresses you as a father addresses his son? It says,

'My son, do not make light of the Lord's discipline,
     and do not lose heart when he rebukes you,
because the Lord disciplines the one he loves,
     and he chastens everyone he accepts as his son.'

Endure hardship as discipline; God is treating you as his children. For what children are not disciplined by their father? If you are not disciplined – and everyone undergoes discipline – then you are not legitimate, not true sons and daughters at all. Moreover, we have all had human fathers who disciplined us and we respected them for it. How much more should we submit to the Father of spirits and live! They disciplined us for a little while as they thought best; but God disciplines us for our good, in order that we may share in his holiness. No discipline seems pleasant at the time, but painful. Later on, however, it produces a harvest of righteousness and peace for those who have been trained by it.

Therefore, strengthen your feeble arms and weak knees. 'Make level paths for your feet,' so that the lame may not be disabled, but rather healed.
(Hebrews 12:4–13)

He makes three points.

1. Suffering as a proof of sonship

God has not deserted us, nor is he displeased with us. It is easy to think that God is either angry or that he simply doesn't care. We take suffering to be an indication of an absence of love.

But the author challenges this false conclusion in verses 5–8. This common error is the result of spiritual amnesia. The people have forgotten what the Bible teaches. He reminds them of Proverbs 3:12:

> . . . the LORD disciplines those he loves,
>   as a father the son he delights in.

Jesus learned obedience through what he suffered (Hebrews 5:8). Why are we so surprised that we need to do the same?

He drives home his point in two statements, one positive and one negative. They should endure hardship and see it as discipline, because God is treating them as sons (12:7). A father who cares will love his children enough to seek to shape their character through discipline. In case they have missed his point, he makes it again, but this time in negative terms (12:8). The time to worry is not when we suffer but, ironically, when we don't! Suffering in the life of the disciple is sure evidence that God is our Father and that he loves us deeply.

Jesus learned obedience through what he suffered (Hebrews 5:8). Why are we so surprised that we need to do the same?

It may seem that he is labouring his point, but that is because it is all too easy to forget it. The natural human reaction to pain is to see it as a sign of divine displeasure or parental neglect. If God loved me, then why would he send this? The answer is indeed counter-intuitive: he has sent it because he *does* love you.

When my boys were small, I used to discipline them when they needed it. After the punishment had been administered, they were sent to their bedroom to think about it. After a while,

I would go and talk to them, and we would have a kind of post-match debriefing. I would sit them on my lap and ask them why Dad had punished them. They would answer me through their tears:

'It's because . . . [sob] . . . you love us . . . [sob] . . . and you want us to be . . . [sob] . . . the best little boys we can be.'

They understood the theory – even though they may not have been entirely convinced by its execution!

Good parents love their kids enough to teach them the difference between right and wrong. They help them to understand that there are consequences for bad behaviour. When God chastens us, it is not necessarily because we have sinned, but it is always a sign that he loves us. It is an unloving parent who fails to discipline. And God is certainly not an unloving parent.

Like a perfect Father, he will never let you go, he will never let you down, but, if you do wrong, he will never let you off.

2. In the hands of the perfect Father

Then, the writer of Hebrews takes us a little further (12:9–10).

The second point he wants his readers to see is that their trials come from the hand of a perfect Father. In their case, it was persecution. They had not yet had to shed their blood (12:4), but the suffering had been pretty severe. In such circumstances, it is tempting to think that these trials are beyond the orbit of God's control. As we have already seen, this is both unhelpful and unbiblical. We affirm human responsibility, but we also affirm God's ultimate control of everything that goes on. The writer has already insisted that the adverse circumstances have come from the hand of their loving Father (12:5–8). He now reminds them that it is the 'Father of [our] spirits' who is doing this (12:9), and doing it for our good (12:10).

Why does he make this point so forcibly? Because he wants them to trust that God knows exactly what he is doing.

Think of the contrast with earthly fathers. They usually mean well but sometimes get it wrong. As a dad, I always tried to make the punishment fit the crime. But sometimes I got it wrong. There were times when the punishment was disproportionate. There were even times when I punished the wrong criminal! Sometimes, I was too severe. Sometimes, I was too indulgent. When I realized I had made a mistake, I always apologized. My kids always forgave me, because they knew I loved them and that I would never willingly or without good reason deliberately make them unhappy.

The point in these verses is that we respect imperfect earthly parents who might make mistakes. How much more should we respect and trust our heavenly Father who never makes mistakes? God is all-loving; he never hurts us unduly. God is all-powerful; his discipline is never out of control. God is all-wise; he never makes a mistake. His discipline is always perfectly designed to achieve his purpose in our lives. He never tests us beyond our ability to endure. He never acts out of spite or anger, like some earthly parents do. The punishment always fits the crime, and he always identifies the true criminal!

These verses are reminiscent of Romans 8:28–29:

> And we know that in all things God works for the good of those who love him, who have been called according to his purpose.
> For those God foreknew he also predestined to be conformed to the image of his Son, that he might be the firstborn among many brothers and sisters.
> (Romans 8:28–29)

What we think is good may not be the same as what God thinks of as good. We perhaps think that what we really need is comfort and tranquillity. God knows that the real good we need is to be conformed to the image of his Son, that we should bear the family likeness.

This leads on to the last point.

3. Our Father knows what he is doing

We are sometimes mystified by suffering. We just don't get it. But our Father knows exactly. He disciplines us so that we will be like Jesus, so that we will be holy (Hebrews 12:10). As a result of this, we can be confident that, one day, this discipline will yield the fruit that God is expecting (12:11).

In a change of metaphor, the author compares God to a farmer who works hard to prepare the ground and plant his crop. It is back-breaking work, but the day comes when the ground yields a bumper harvest and the farmer realizes that all his labour was worth it. In the same way, God sows pain so that one day there will be a harvest of righteousness and peace. The fruit of the Spirit (Galatians 5:22–23) grows only in the ground that has been broken up with the plough of pain.

Keep on running!

In the last couple of verses (Hebrews 12:12–13), he returns to the metaphor of the runner with which he began the chapter. Marathon runners will tell you that sometimes it is in the middle of a race that they hit the pain barrier. They have gone so far, but there is still a long way to go, and they feel like giving up.

This is also true when we suffer, especially when that suffering is chronic. There have been times over the last twenty years when Edrie has felt like giving up – and so have I. How much more pain can she take? How much more suffering is necessary to achieve God's purpose? Like the marathon runner, arms feel feeble and knees begin to buckle. What do we do in such circumstances? Persevere and don't give up (12:1). Keep your eyes on Jesus who finished the race (12:2–3).Trust the fact that your heavenly Father loves you (12:4–9). Recognize that God is treating you as his child (12:7–8). Submit to him because he does not make mistakes (12:9–10). Look for the bumper harvest that is bound to come (12:11). Just keep going (12:12–13).

The family likeness

Emmaus, the baby born in adversity, is now twenty years old. A couple of weeks ago, she took her mum with her to buy her wedding dress. I sat in a coffee shop and worked until they had completed their search. I then went to pay for the dress – dads do have their uses.

When I arrived at the bridal store, they took me into the fitting room where Emmaus was still wearing the dress she had chosen. She turned to smile at me, and the resemblance to her mum was uncanny. I was reminded of the day almost thirty-four years ago when I turned and saw my beautiful bride walk down the aisle and into my arms.

When we make our marriage vows, most of us really have no idea what 'for better or worse; for richer, for poorer; in sickness and health . . .' really will mean. It's probably a good thing too.

Emmaus looks like her mum. I like to think that, during her life, she will show the same courage and patient determination. I hope that she might also have inherited some of my better characteristics. We all carry the family likeness in some way or another. Through the painful experiences of this life, God is stamping his family likeness upon us. And like Jesus, we are learning obedience through our suffering.

8. Reasons to be cheerful

Minor triumphs

Come back with me to our main story.

People said that, after Emmaus was born, Edrie would quickly get better. The neurologist blitzed her with a strong course of steroids. (Edrie wept, although she recognized the wisdom of it, because she realized that she would be deprived of the joy of feeding Emmaus herself.) But there seemed to be no significant improvement. I visited the hospital every day. I introduced Emmaus to her brothers and sister.

The kids had been amazing. We decided that I would take them over to see their mum every other day. In between, friends from church looked after them and they enjoyed all the attention and special treats. I would try to get home before bedtime to pray with them each night. It was good to remember their concerns, and particularly their mum. Caleb was ten, Amos eight and Keziah five. They were remarkably brave and seemed to take it all in their stride. We had been worried about the impact on them, particularly if Edrie did not improve, but they were all doing well.

As I said earlier, our prayers began to focus on two things. Firstly, we wanted our baby to be well. Secondly, we prayed that, when the time came, Mum would be able to walk into our home carrying their new sister in her arms. That may seem a strange prayer, but I think we were coming to terms with the fact that Mum might never be quite the same again. We were not demanding that God would fully heal her, but that there might be some normality about our lives.

So Emmaus got to meet her siblings. She was actually born on Amos's birthday, so we made a lot of that. The boys and Keziah loved her at first sight and fought over who got to hold her the longest. Edrie was still exhausted, but she put on her make-up and a brave face, and we tried to be as normal as possible.

Over the next few years, we would guard our family life so that Edrie's illness did not come to define us as a family. Of course, there would be things that Mum could not do, but she would try to make things as normal as possible. The kids would be fiercely loyal and ferociously protective. They would be proud of Mum's courage, and woe betide anyone who 'dissed' her.

But for now, in the hospital, our now-complete family unit bonded well and we thanked God that he had answered the first of our prayers. Emmaus was indeed healthy and well.

Edrie stayed in hospital for another couple of weeks. Messages of congratulations flooded in. Again, we heard from people we had never met, assuring us that they had not stopped praying and that they shared our joy. I was moved by a note from a pastor's wife who knew neither Edrie nor me, but who informed me that the ladies in the church had held special prayer meetings for us.

The steroids still didn't seem to be taking effect, but Edrie was growing stronger. Her balance had not returned and her speech was still slurred, but she was determined that she would do everything in her power to be as normal as possible. I took her for a walk in the hospital grounds, and we thanked God for his amazing goodness to us.

The day finally arrived. Edrie had been in hospital for almost three months. A nurse carried Emmaus to the car and handed her over to Edrie in the passenger seat. I drove home carefully but excitedly. The kids had made a banner to welcome us. And Edrie walked into our home carrying Emmaus! It was a very slow walk, and I held her up the whole way, but she did manage it.

'And now,' she said, 'I want a real cup of tea!'

Home at last

Over the next few weeks, Edrie needed to convalesce. Her dad came up with a perfect solution. He would come and live in our home and look after our children and, for the next two weeks, Edrie, Emmaus and I would move over to his bungalow. The kids adored Grampie and were very enthusiastic about this. I wasn't so sure at first, but it soon became clear that Edrie would need careful nursing. So we accepted the perfect solution.

The church insisted that I take off the next two weeks – very fortunate, because paternity leave was not so common twenty years ago. We moved into the bungalow, which was also called 'Emmaus', I looked after my girls, and things were good.

Each day, I would attend to Edrie's needs and try to find little treats to give her. I would feed Emmaus and make sure she was happy. It was a new experience for me – we had never needed to use a bottle before. I remember being terrified by the health visitor. I could cope with abstract theology and obscure exegesis, but I could never remember the order in which you put the hot water and the milk powder into the bottle. But Emmaus survived – more than that, she seemed to flourish. God had blessed us with a really contented baby. It was during those two weeks that she began to sleep through most of the night. She was never fractious, and we were so grateful.

The church had arranged a rota, and people delivered a meal every day. Grampie brought the kids every afternoon after school. They were having a great time and couldn't wait to tell us what treats Edrie's dad had showered on them: 'Today he did a smiley face in bacon and eggs and hash browns for breakfast – why don't you ever do that?'

I look back on that time as idyllic. Every day, we had time to talk and pray and thank God for his bountiful kindness. In the afternoons, we went for walks. It was a little awkward at first – how *do* you push a wheelchair and a pram at the same time? But we fixed it so that Edrie would hold Emmaus very carefully and I would push her chair. We went out with increasing confidence and looked forward to what seemed to symbolize for us a kind of return to normality. The sun seemed to shine every day that summer. Life was good.

Counting blessings

Life is about giving things back. At the start of our lives, most of us are given a full set of faculties and opportunities. As we go on, we may get showered with other blessings too. But in the normal course of most lives, we reach the moment when we have to start giving things back. It starts with little things: we can no longer read unaided by glasses; we find we have less breath after we have climbed the stairs; we just don't sleep as well as we used to. As we get older, other complications arrive. Young doctors tell us that it is only to be expected.

And then it gets really serious. The list of things that once were easy becomes the list of things that are no longer attainable. What we could once take in our stride becomes a mountain too high to climb.

And then we lose people. People are the most precious gifts God gives us – and it's really hard to give them back. For many of us, the greatest gift is a life partner. When God gives a man a wife, he gives him a good thing. When he takes the gift back, it is the deepest shock that flesh is heir to.

It is right to grieve over the things we have lost, but the secret of enduring joy is not to dwell on those things. Yes, grieve over what is lost, but dwell on what is left and what can never be lost. In the words of the old hymn, 'Count your blessings, name them one by one, and it will surprise you what the Lord has done.'

During those idyllic summer days just after Emmaus was born, Edrie and I thought about what God had given us, rather than what he had taken away. We still had each other. We had a beautiful baby to complete our family. We had close relatives who loved us and were there for us. We had a great church who loved and cared for us. It looked as if I was going to be able to continue as pastor after all. The sun was shining, and the food was good! Over and beyond that, we were Christians and God loved us and promised that he would never let us go.

Joy is very much an attitude of heart and a decision of faith.

Joy is very much an attitude of heart and a decision of faith. We can constantly grieve over what we have lost, or we can rejoice in what we have. My advice to you is: choose joy!

Another psalm

During those weeks at Grampie's, we discovered Psalm 103.

Many of the psalms are passionate cries of faith and requests for deliverance from adverse circumstances. But Psalm 103 contains no entreaties or appeals for help – it is a request-free zone. It is an expression of praise and gratitude for God's amazing grace and undeserved kindness.

The psalm is divided into three parts. In a short introduction (103:1–5), David reflects on his personal reasons to praise God. In the long central section (103:6–18), he looks back on the blessings that God has poured upon his people during their long and eventful history. In the short conclusion (103:19–22), he calls on the whole of creation – visible and invisible – to praise God. It encourages us all to count our blessings and to dwell on God's grace.

Personal praise

Do you ever talk to yourself? Well, Psalm 103 begins with David doing just that. Twice he calls on his soul to praise God. He takes himself by the scruff of the neck and insists on praising God wholeheartedly.

How can we have such an attitude of heart amid the struggles of everyday life? David gives the answer in verse 2: '. . . and forget not all his benefits' (103:2).

The secret of permanent praise is sanctified memory. We have to choose to call to mind God's blessings, rather than dwell on our trials and troubles. We find it easier to complain about a few fleeting troubles than to remember mountains of mercies. We wallow in sorrow rather than swimming in the depths of God's goodness. The great Baptist preacher Charles Haddon Spurgeon put it like this: 'We write our blessings in the sand; we carve our complaints in marble.'

David will have none of this. In the next three verses, he reminds himself of five blessings which God has poured into his life.

So many blessings

Firstly, God forgives all our sins (103:3). It is no surprise that David begins here. This is the first and fundamental and fountain-head blessing. Every other blessing flows from this. In mid-life, David had committed a terrible sin by taking the wife of another man and then arranging for the wronged man to be killed. When

David came to his senses, the effects of his guilt threatened to destroy him.

Then came the moment when he received God's forgiveness! He was overwhelmed with gratitude and expressed himself in superlative terms:

> Blessed is the one
>> whose transgressions are forgiven,
>> whose sins are covered.
> Blessed is the one
>> whose sin the LORD does not count against them
>> and in whose spirit is no deceit.
> (Psalm 32:1–2)

A relationship with God always begins with forgiveness. Whatever adverse conditions we may pass through, we belong to the fellowship of the forgiven, and this should cause us to praise God every day of our lives. Don't ever forget that!

Secondly, David confesses that the Lord 'heals all your diseases' (103:3). This is a little more tricksy. This verse has been quoted at me several times by those who tell me that Edrie should not be sick. ' "All diseases" means "all diseases",' they have insisted. How do we respond?

It is helpful to remember that David was writing during the days of the Mosaic covenant. Under that covenant, sin was sometimes punished with sickness, and repentance was often marked by healing. When David repented of his sin, God healed him. But we are in the new covenant, which does not promise physical healing here and now.

Of course, God can heal if he chooses to. He may do it miraculously or by using more mundane methods. But whether the source of healing is miraculous or medical or natural, all health comes from God and we should be grateful for it. We also need to remember that, one day, God will heal us totally. One day, Edrie will be 'raised immortal'. If God does not choose to heal her now, we can rejoice in anticipation of that day. Remember that!

Thirdly, David remembers that God 'redeems your life from the pit' (103:4). In our own stupidity and waywardness, we often dig a pit and then fall into it. That is what David has done. Much of the suffering in the latter part of his life was down to his own mistakes. However, when he cried out to God, God delivered him. God delivers us too from the consequences of our folly, over and over again. We don't deserve it, but he does it nonetheless. This is another motive for praise. Remember that!

Fourthly, David reminds us that God 'crowns you with love and compassion' (103:4). He lavishes the blessings of salvation on us. Like a crown of glory, God places the crown of grace on his children. Remember that!

Finally, God 'satisfies your desires with good things so that your youth is renewed like the eagle's' (103:5). When we come to experience God's grace, we come to understand that God has rescued us for a relationship. The greatest blessing of the gospel is God himself. Listen to David in Psalm 27:

> One thing I ask from the LORD,
>   this only do I seek:
> that I may dwell in the house of the LORD
>   all the days of my life,
> to gaze on the beauty of the LORD
>   and to seek him in his temple.
> (Psalm 27:4)

The greatest blessing we have is that this God is our God forever. Meditating on this leads to spiritual renewal, so that, like the desert eagle which sheds its old plumage and appears to be young again, we can find the secret of 'eternal spiritual youthfulness' when we dwell on the knowledge of God.

Remember that!

The glorious galaxy of grace

In the second part of the psalm, we move from the individual to the corporate, from the singular to the plural (103:6–18). As he reflects on history, David is overwhelmed by the greatness of the grace of God. In a kaleidoscopic description, he speaks of the glorious galaxy of grace.

He speaks of this grace in three dimensions.

Past grace

Firstly, he reminds the people of past grace (103:6–12). During the whole of their history, God was gracious to them, an un-deserving nation. When they cried out to him from the slavery and oppression of Egypt, he rescued them (verse 6). He led them to Mount Sinai, where he entered into a covenant with them. Like a marriage, this was to be an exclusive and intimate rela-tionship. God opened his heart and revealed his ways to them (verse 7).

God's amazing grace had redeemed them, he had brought them to himself and had called them to be his people in a dark world, bearing testimony to him. They were a 'kingdom of priests and a holy nation'. You might expect that this would have secured their perpetual faithfulness. But, as we saw earlier, within forty days, they had broken the covenant (Exodus 32). This was more than a breach of law; it was an act of spiritual adultery. It might well have been the end of the line, but instead God was determined to have mercy. He renewed his covenant and revealed the glory of his grace to Moses:

> Then the LORD came down in the cloud and stood there
> with him and proclaimed his name, the LORD. And he passed
> in front of Moses, proclaiming, 'The LORD, the LORD, the
> compassionate and gracious God, slow to anger, abounding
> in love and faithfulness, maintaining love to thousands, and
> forgiving wickedness, rebellion and sin. Yet he does not leave

the guilty unpunished; he punishes the children and their
children for the sin of the parents to the third and fourth
generation.
(Exodus 34:5–7)

David alludes to this in verse 8 of Psalm 103. God does not treat
us as we deserve. During their history, Israel constantly tested
God's patience, but they constantly discovered his grace. David
magnifies this past experience of grace:

> The LORD is compassionate and gracious,
>> slow to anger, abounding in love.
> He will not always accuse,
>> nor will he harbour his anger for ever;
> he does not treat us as our sins deserve
>> or repay us according to our iniquities.
> For as high as the heavens are above the earth,
>> so great is his love for those who fear him;
> as far as the east is from the west,
>> so far has he removed our transgressions from us.
> (Psalm 103:8–12)

We need to hear this today. Too often we think that God is mean
and parsimonious. We imagine that he is watching us carefully and waiting for us to step out of line so that he can zap us.
We think of a God who, to paraphrase, is 'slow to mercy and
quick to anger'.

But God is not an overbearing sergeant major nor a fierce head
teacher. The God who rescued Israel delights to have mercy. He
takes pleasure in putting our sins behind his back and remembering them no more.

When we suffer, we need to find comfort in the knowledge
that there is nothing we can do to make him love us more and
nothing we can do to make him love us less. The great Puritan
theologian John Owen put it like this: 'The greatest sorrow or

burden you can lay on the Father – the greatest unkindness you can do him is to not believe that he loves you.'[1]

Present grace
In the next section of the psalm, David reminds us of God's unchanging fatherly love:

> As a father has compassion on his children,
>> so the LORD has compassion on those who fear him;
> for he knows how we are formed,
>> he remembers that we are dust.
>
> (Psalm 103:13–14)

When the Bible compares God to a father, it often reminds us that, like a father, God protects and provides, guides and disciplines. But here the emphasis is on the tenderness and intimacy of a father's love.

In 2012, our elder daughter Keziah had a baby. Edrie and I visited Avennah when she was just two days old, and Kez was holding her. Kez asked Matt, her husband, to take his daughter for a moment. Now Matt is a big bearded Welshman. He approached with a look of adoration and anxiety. Avennah was indeed tiny, like a little hedgehog. He took her tenderly into his strong embrace. At that moment, I looked at him looking at her and thought, poor bloke – he's caught. He will love this little scrap of life for the rest of his days. He will be excited by her first steps and boast of her first words. When she cries, he will soothe her and, when she is in need, he will always be there for her. One day, he may have that bitter-sweet experience of walking her down the aisle and placing her hand in the hand of another man – someone once described this experience as akin to taking a priceless antique Stradivarius violin and putting it in the hands of a gorilla.

Why will this love never change? Because he will remember those moments when she lay so weak and frail and vulnerable in his arms. That is a picture of God's gracious attitude towards us. He does not set unrealistic goals. He does not make unreasonable demands. His love does not depend on our performance or our achievements. He knows all our weaknesses and he loves us all the same. This grace and loving-kindness is tender and gentle, compassionate and warm. Such is his present grace.

Future grace

David then reminds us of God's future grace. Human life is frail and fleeting, like the grass that withers and dies. We are here for a moment and then we are gone (103:15–16). But God's grace is different:

> But from everlasting to everlasting
> the LORD's love is with those who fear him,
> and his righteousness with their children's children –
> with those who keep his covenant
> and remember to obey his precepts.
> (103:17–18)

He loved us before the world began. He will love us until the world is no more. His love will never stop and his grace will never fail. If we are Christians, we are in Christ, and God will always love us because he loves Christ and he sees us in him. How can we fail to have grateful hearts when we think about this amazing grace?

Universal praise

In the final part of the psalm, David calls on the whole creation to worship God. This God of grace is not a weak and helpless deity – he is the Lord whose throne is established forever and whose universal kingdom cannot fail (103:19).

David summons the angels to praise their Creator. We sometimes trivialize angels and forget that they are 'mighty ones who do his bidding'. Were we to see an angel, we would be overwhelmed by his majesty and probably tempted to worship him. At the same time, angels are only 'servants who do his will' (103:20–21). Their whole purpose in existing is to praise God; they are designed for adoration.

From the angels, he turns to the material creation:

> Praise the LORD, all his works
>> everywhere in his dominion.
> (103:22)

All that God has made should bring him praise. The purpose and end of the material universe is to bring glory to its Creator.

And David ends where he began:

> Praise the LORD, my soul.
> (103:22)

Which will you choose?

Life is about making choices.

We can choose to grieve over what we have lost, to complain about our disappointments and grumble about our hardships. Or we can rejoice in the treasures of God's grace and celebrate his bountiful gifts. We can delight in every good thing he has poured into our lives.

David goes out of his way deliberately to remember the entirety of what God has done for him personally, for his people historically and for the world universally.

During those warm summer days, Edrie and I had a sense of overwhelming gratitude. God had been so good to us. We experienced deep, healing joy. We chose to remember what we still had, not what we had lost.

You can do the same. The choice is yours. Which will you choose?

9. Living with uncertainty

During the first few months after the birth of Emmaus, we were content just to have got through the ordeal and be back together as a family. After two weeks in the bungalow, we returned to our own home, and life began to settle into some kind of routine.

The summer came to an end. I went back to work. The kids went back to school. Edrie began to explore what she could do within the confines of her new limitations. We all agreed that the first meal she cooked was one of the best we had ever eaten. She discovered that, if she was careful, she could do some jobs around the house. We went back to church, and there was great jubilation on the first Sunday that we all arrived as a family.

We had regular appointments with the neurologist and further tests – more MRI scans and yet another dreaded lumbar puncture.

As time went by and life became more normal, we began to ask more and more questions. What was actually wrong with Edrie? What had brought this on? How would it develop? Could we expect her to get better? All good questions – but no-one seemed to have answers. The neurologist referred us to another specialist. He was convinced that it was multiple sclerosis, even though some of the normal symptoms were missing. Our own doctor was not convinced. Still the questions hovered in our heads.

A bit of an adventure

We shared our struggles for prayer at church, and one day one of our men came to see us. He was concerned and wanted to help. He had done some research and discovered that the best neurological facility in the country was at the University of Central London Institute of Neurology in Queen Square. He wanted to pay for us to visit the institute and have a consultation with the top UK specialist.

We were in two minds. It would mean a trip to London. We had confidence in the neurologists we had seen – what could this new guy tell us? On the other hand, we didn't want to spurn our friend's generosity and it would all be a bit of an adventure. What decided things was curiosity – we really wanted a diagnosis. If we passed up this opportunity, we would probably regret it in the future.

So we made the pilgrimage up to the big city. An Anglican friend arranged for us to use his flat overnight. It was a bit of a jaunt. We arrived the day before the appointment and got to see some of the sights. We had a romantic meal in a little restaurant and prepared for the next day.

Travelling on the underground was a nightmare. At this stage, Edrie was able to walk short distances, as long as I was with her. But, on the escalator down into the bowels of the city, I had to stand next to her to prevent her from falling. We had several unhelpful comments from commuters who were unhappy that we were blocking their route. I found myself becoming pretty irate, but, as usual, Edrie was her sedate and calm self.

We made it to the hospital with an hour to spare. As it was a private consultation, they plied us with tea and biscuits as soporific classical music played soothingly in the background.

Eventually, we got to see the consultant. He was a professor at the university and had a reputation as one of the best diagnosticians in the world. He had just returned from a lecture series overseas. This guy really was the end of the line in the diagnosis of neurological conditions.

He spent an hour with Edrie. He asked her questions; he asked me questions. He did some of the standard tests. He watched her walk. He examined her three MRI scan results and the results of her lumbar punctures.

After an hour, he gave us his considered opinion. He was fairly convinced that Edrie did not have MS. Many of the symptoms were similar, but the scans and tests did not fit. As to an actual diagnosis, he told us that it was unlike anything he had ever met before. The most likely verdict was that she had a genetic abnormality that had lain dormant until the pregnancy. The changes to her body, brought on by the pregnancy, had triggered it. It had been like a time bomb waiting to go off. So the pregnancy had activated this condition. He could not give her a diagnosis and therefore could not give her a prognosis.

He reassured us that this was not unusual, and that he regularly gave similar news to patients who had been referred to him after a lack of diagnosis. Edrie's details would be fed into a computer somewhere, and one day a pattern might emerge, and it might be possible to put a name to her condition. Perhaps one day, someone somewhere might even come up with a viable treatment. We needed to wait for a phone call that would tell us of this breakthrough.

That was almost twenty years ago. We are still waiting for that phone call.

Fearfully and wonderfully made

Our response was mixed. On the one hand, we were disappointed. Obviously. We had really hoped for a diagnosis, hoped that we would come away with a treatment that would make Edrie better. And both hopes were now dashed.

On the other hand, we now knew that we had done everything that human intuition and God-given wisdom could possibly do to find a solution. It is spiritual arrogance to ignore medical help when it is available. God had given skill to the neurologists and gynaecologists who had been such a help to Edrie. Theologians call it 'common grace': the good gifts that God delights to give to all people. Over the years, Edrie would consult with speech therapists, physiotherapists and occupational therapists. They have all helped in one way or another, and we are indeed grateful. But, ultimately, we were and are in God's hands.

After our London visit, I set myself the task of finding out as much as I could about the nature of the human brain. Its intricacies have puzzled and baffled people throughout the ages. I discovered that the average brain weighs only about three pounds, and your skin is twice the weight of this. The brain is made up of grey matter (Hercule Poirot's 'little grey cells') or neurons, which gather and transmit signals. There is also white matter composed of dendrites and axons. These form the network which the neurons use to send their signals. And, amazingly, 75% of your brain is composed of water.[1]

The brain is actually made up of around 100 billion neurons, about the same number of stars as are in the Milky Way. I have also read that there are as many neurons as there are trees in the Amazon rainforest. They are connected by synapses. There are anywhere from 1,000 to 10,000 synapses for each neuron. And there are as many synapses in the brain as there are leaves on the trees of the Brazilian rainforest (although some of us might feel that autumn has arrived early!). There are 100,000 miles of blood vessels in the brain, but no pain receptors, so it can feel no pain. The brain uses 20% of the total oxygen in your body. It can live for four to six minutes without oxygen, and then it begins to die. An absence of oxygen for five to ten minutes will result in permanent brain damage.

Other things I have learned . . .

You can't tickle yourself, because the brain makes a distinction between unexpected external touch and your own touch. Our sense of smell is the strongest one at creating and evoking memories. My wife used to apply a perfume called Charlie when we were courting. It was considered a sophisticated fragrance in those days. When I smell it almost forty years later, I am a young man again! That's the power of the brain for you.

Neurologists and brain surgeons have been studying the brain for the best part of a hundred years. At Harvard Medical School there is a 'brain bank' with more than 7,000 human brains on deposit – I'm not sure how you make a withdrawal. And something like 70,000 thoughts pass through our brains in a single day.[2]

All these things I discovered during my research.

I also discovered that scientists are more mystified by the brain than by any other organ in the human body. We know more about outer space than inner space. We are indeed fearfully and wonderfully made.

View from the balloon

During Edrie's time in hospital, we had been wonderfully supported by the church I pastored, Ladyfield Evangelical in Chippenham, Wiltshire. People visited and prayed and sent encouragements and food. Our deep freeze was full of quiches – standard Christian fare! In particular, the young people were wonderfully supportive. Many of them had come to Christ during my ministry and they just wanted to show us how much they loved us.

When I returned to work, the church continued to be fantastic. At first, they wanted to wrap us in cotton wool. But, as I said earlier, we wanted things to get back to normal, so, within a couple of months, I was back in full swing, preaching two or three times a week and taking a full load of pastoral care. Edrie was severely restricted, but she managed to keep things together at home. I felt supported and carried along by her faithful prayer ministry; I may have been in the pulpit, but it seemed that it was Edrie who kept me there. To this day, I often describe her as my secret weapon.

It was then that the young people came to tell us that they had a gift for us. Edrie had been in hospital in Bath. When she had looked out of the window, she had been able to see hot air balloons drifting across the horizon. In her long and painful confinement, these symbolized freedom and a future. The young people had picked up on this and had clubbed together to send us on a balloon ride across Bath.

The day for our flight arrived – it had been postponed once because of adverse weather conditions. Lots of young people turned up to see us off – some even wanted to follow us in their cars. When we were still on the ground, I asked our pilot how far we would go and which direction we would follow.

He smiled at my naivety: 'I have no idea. We are dependent on the wind. We go in the direction and at the speed that it takes us.'

That didn't particularly inspire confidence, but he seemed to know what he was doing.

Eventually, we left the ground. We soared over the old Roman city and gazed down on its beautiful aquatint Georgian buildings. As we drifted in the direction of the hospital, I tried to identify Edrie's room, but we did not get close enough. Then the wind wafted us away from the city and towards the countryside. To me, this was the most revealing aspect of balloon flight. I had been up in a plane, but it is so far up and you are so closed in that you feel you have no connection with the earth so far below. A balloon is much, much closer to the ground. What is more, you are not enclosed in the same way as in an aeroplane, but can see things at short range. Most significantly of all, a balloon is almost silent. As we floated over the fields, I could see our shadow making its stately progress. I could also see animals who were totally oblivious to, and undisturbed by, our presence. Not just cows and sheep, but also a couple of foxes and one deer. They didn't even lift their heads to look in our direction. If Edrie had experienced a serenity and freedom watching the balloons from her hospital bed, then there was an even more profound serenity and peace to be had from looking down on the world from the balloon basket.

Eventually, we returned to terra firma. As I reflected on our aerial adventure, it seemed to be a kind of parable of our condition.

I recognized two parallels.

1. Handing over your life to another

We were putting ourselves into the hands of our balloonist, and he was putting himself in the hands of the airstream. At the hospital, we had put ourselves in the hands of the neurologist and trusted him to help us. In each case, our trust had been well placed. Our pilot landed us safely, and the doctors had done everything in their power to help.

But now we were in a situation in which medical science could take us no further. We had exhausted its resources. I don't say that in any belligerent way. As you know, I was grateful for everything. But now one of the best neurologists in the land was stumped. What was left?

We had to trust God. I am not suggesting that that was our last resort; we had tried to trust God all the way through. But now we were in the situation where our future was entirely in his hands. This future is unknown terrain, and like our balloon at the mercy of the wind, we have to go in the direction and at the pace that God takes us. Faith involves handing our future to God. We have to surrender to our heavenly Father, trusting him to take care of our journey. Just because the wind might have taken us in a direction that we didn't expect or anticipate was no reason to stop trusting.

Edrie and I felt as if we had been carried on strange winds and blown to unforeseen places. But isn't that what it means to affirm that Jesus is Lord and to give your life to him? Christianity involves surrendering everything to God. Some people once asked the evangelist Rodney 'Gypsy' Smith how they might experience the same revival as he had. He replied, 'Go home. Lock yourself in your room. Kneel down in the middle of the floor, and with a piece of chalk draw a circle round yourself. There, on your knees, pray fervently and brokenly that God would start a revival within that chalk circle.'[3]

Edrie and I felt as if we had been carried on strange winds and blown to unforeseen places.

He was right.

God wants us to trust him when we cannot see the way. That means leaving our concerns at his feet. He is never reluctant to carry our cares for us. The psalmist expresses it in this way:

> His pleasure is not in the strength of the horse,
>   nor his delight in the legs of the warrior;
> the LORD delights in those who fear him,
>   who put their hope in his unfailing love.
> (Psalm 147:10–11)

In the cut and thrust of the history of Israel, there were many times when the nation faced overwhelming odds. In such circumstances, it was tempting to trust in their own armies or to turn for support to one of their neighbours (the 'strength of the horse' and the 'legs of the warrior'). But this was always a mistake. God challenged his people to trust him alone.

He goes further than this. God actually *delights* in us when we fear him and trust him.

I find this incredibly encouraging. There are many things we cannot do. Most of us feel we are making slow progress in our Christian lives and we are often aware of our besetting failures. We do not love God as we think we ought to love him; we still make stupid mistakes; we let the Lord down. What can I do to delight the Lord? The answer is that he delights in those who, in childlike faith, cast themselves at his feet and seek to trust him alone. There are lots of things I cannot do, but I can do that! And sometimes that is all God wants. We are saved by abandoning ourselves to him and trusting in all that Jesus did for us. That is the way in which we are to live our lives every day.

Trusting God alone

There is a story about the time when Hudson Taylor was preparing to go to inland China as a pioneer missionary.[4] He was telling a group of his supporters that the way ahead was unclear to him. He would be beyond the reach of human help and support. Reflecting on this, one of his friends was heard to remark: 'Poor Hudson Taylor; when he gets to China, he will have no-one to help him. He will be forced to trust in God alone.'

> *Hudson Taylor had to learn to trust in God alone.*

I wonder whether the irony of his remark ever dawned on him!

Hudson Taylor had to learn to trust in God alone. Our circumstance had forced Edrie and me to do the same.

But that is the position we are all in. For example, whether or not you live to finish reading this book is out of your control. Stop reading and feel your pulse. Can you find it? If not, you are in trouble! The heart of the average person beats around 36,000,000 times a year. That amounts to around 2,520,000,000 times in seventy years.[5] And every heartbeat is a gift from God!

Just over a year ago, I preached at a church in Wiltshire. Edrie and I were returning home in the dark afterwards. We were just approaching Royal Wootton Bassett when Edrie let out a scream. A car, travelling at breakneck speed, was heading directly for us on the wrong side of the road. I took evasive action and narrowly avoided a head-on collision, but the driver hit us in the side and spun us round. We landed in a ditch. The air-bags exploded and the car was filled with the smell of cordite . . . After a great deal of loud noise, silence fell.

Then Edrie spoke.

'Are you alive?' she said.

'Yes,' I replied, 'Are you?'

She did not answer this slightly redundant question. Instead, after a few heartbeats, she said, 'You are going to get so many sermon illustrations from this, aren't you?'

How well she knows me!

So here is one: our lives are totally in the hands of another. We never know what is round each (literal) bend in the road. We do not know which way the wind will blow our balloon. And we never know what strange providences God has planned for us.

We are at the mercy of something beyond ourselves. But here is the difference: we are not in the hands of an erratic late-night driver or unpredictable meteorological conditions. We are in the hands of a God who loves us more than we can imagine, One who proved it by sending his Son to die for us.

2. Looking down from above

The second lesson from our aerial expedition was that things always look different from above.

Looking down from the balloon's basket, there is noise and bustle. Up above is peace and serenity. We are so often trapped into the here and now. Life is so overwhelming that we never get to lift up our eyes and see God's big picture. It is all a matter of perspective. We cannot live our lives up above the world, looking down from the balloon's basket. We have to live in the cut and thrust of everyday life, getting our hands dirty down on the ground. Indeed, that is where God wants us to be.

But sometimes, we need to soar above our everyday experience and look down on things from heaven's perspective.

After the failure to diagnose Edrie's illness, that was exactly what we needed. Travelling home from London by train, we had talked about it. Edrie was feeling pretty low. She had had high hopes and now felt totally deflated. I tried to encourage her, but it didn't work. We lived under a cloud of depression for a couple of days. But it didn't last. By the end of the week, Edrie was back to her cheerful, courageous self.

What made the difference? We had climbed some hills near our home, the Lickey Hills to the south of Birmingham. My dad had taken me there on bank holidays when I was a kid. I remember walking across the hills, wearing my Davy Crockett hat and singing 'King of the Wild Frontier'. Our church youth group used to hold midnight sausage sizzles there (usually finishing around 9pm!). On a cold winter's day in 1978, I had taken Edrie up the Lickeys and, kneeling in the snow, had asked her to be my wife.

So it is a feel-good place for us, and that was where we went to talk and pray. Sitting on the top of the hill, you can see the great city of Birmingham spread out before you, like the New Jerusalem descending from heaven! As we gazed down and prayed about the future, we began to find our faith growing. God helped us to remind ourselves of the big picture, of our motto text: 'As for God, his way is perfect.' God has a plan, and it would not fail. The lack of diagnosis did not frustrate him. Seeing the big picture made all the difference.

Seeing the big picture made all the difference.

The Bible makes it clear that God has a plan for his world, for his church and for every single one of his children. How reassuring is that?

God's plan for the world

God's plan for the world is that one day he will reunite a broken and fractured cosmos under the lordship of Jesus Christ:

> . . . he made known to us the mystery of his will according to his good pleasure, which he purposed in Christ, to be put into effect when the times reach their fulfilment – to bring unity to all things in heaven and on earth under Christ.
> (Ephesians 1:9–10)

The first Adam was created to fill the world and reign over it as God's vice-regent. But he dragged the whole world down with him when he sinned against God in the garden. This cursed world is now divided and damaged and spoilt. The last Adam has been obedient unto death, and, as a result, God has exalted him to his right hand. One day, he will reign over this world. One day, the world will be made whole. Sin and rebellion will be dealt with, and unity will be restored.

When the news bulletins report the latest famine or tsunami or gunman opening fire in a school, and the horrific results leave us sick in the stomach, we need to see the big picture. When good people suffer and bad people flourish and God is mocked or his law flouted or just ignored, we need to see the big picture. When wars and rumours of wars abound or when long-concealed acts of violence against vulnerable children at last become public knowledge, we need to see the big picture.

Jesus will be victorious – the future history of the world has already been written and 'at the name of Jesus every knee should bow' (Philippians 2:10).

God's plan for the church

God also has a plan for his church. It is easy to get depressed about church life, especially if you are working at the coalface in some form of ministry. It often seems to be consumed by petty squabbles and riven by graceless divisions. Some churches work hard at being loving communities, and yet seem too willing to sacrifice objective truth on the altar of utility. Other churches are sounder than the apostles, rigid and cold and as loveless as the grave. There is an ever-growing army of casualties, men and women, who have been 'church-damaged'. Of course, there are some brilliant churches, but even the good ones may feel small and marginal and intimidated when they look at the growing arrogant, militant paganism of the world around them. Let's face it, the church is hardly an army mighty with banners.

It is easy to fall out of love with the church – some Christians even try to go it alone. But that is a mistake. For all its weaknesses, the church is still at the centre of the purposes of God. The church is the bride of Christ, and her destiny is to be glorified and spend eternity with her husband.

I once visited an elderly Christian couple in a care home. I chatted with the husband while his wife slept. When she woke up, she reached for her Zimmer frame. As she slowly crossed the room towards us, with one stocking around her ankle and the marks of sleep still resting in the corners of her eyes, he turned to me, his face suffused with pride:

'That's my girl,' he said in a broad Wiltshire accent. 'Isn't she beautiful?'

It is all a matter of perspective. He saw what I, even in my most chivalrous mood, couldn't see. He loved her and he saw her beauty. Christ loves the church and is preparing an eternity of bliss for her. We need to see the big picture. We need to see the church through the eyes of Christ. You can criticize me; I'm a big boy, and I can cope with it. But you had better not bad-mouth my wife! And you had better not bad-mouth Christ's church either.

One day, God's purpose for his church will reach perfection, and she will be 'without stain or wrinkle or any other blemish, but holy and blameless' (Ephesians 5:27).

That's the big picture, and, in the midst of the battle, we need to remember this.

God's plan for you

God also has a perfect plan for all of his children. We are caught up in the middle of it and so, for much of the time, we cannot see the wood for the trees. Looking down from the hillside as we prayed, we were able, just for a moment, to remember that God knows what he is doing and that we can trust him. We have to live in the valley, but occasionally God lifts us above the strife and reminds us of what he is doing.

At a time of great suffering and trial, the prophet Jeremiah assured God's people that he had not forgotten them. We need to remember the context and not misapply the promise, but, in the broadest possible way, these ancient words of comfort continue to bring comfort to us today:

> 'For I know the plans I have for you,' declares the LORD, 'plans to prosper you and not to harm you, plans to give you hope and a future.'
> (Jeremiah 29:11)

Past grace gives us assurance of future grace. Life is a bit of an adventure. We would love to control the script, but the pen is not in our hands. Accepting the role that God has for us is what it means to be a Christian, what it means to walk by faith. It is what it means to surrender to divine direction and to live for the glory of God.

10. Don't waste your sorrows

After a while, you get used to most things, and what once seemed impossible gradually becomes routine. What you thought was intolerable becomes normal. And so the unbearable in time becomes bearable.

A few years after the onset of Edrie's illness, we had settled into a pattern of acceptance. Life was not what it had been, but, within certain boundaries, we could do most things.

The kids were growing up. Emmaus took her first steps, formed her first words. The boys went to senior school. Caleb became a voracious reader, while Amos excelled at basketball. Keziah took ballet lessons. The children professed faith in Christ. Mum's illness did not seem to wither their faith – instead, with the resilience of children, they came to accept it as a normal part of family life. Church flourished, and we loved and were loved by our Christian family.

However, during this time, Edrie was deteriorating, but it was a very slow and almost imperceptible process.

Then, out of the blue, I received a call to leave Wiltshire and to move up to a church in Worcester. I was a little anxious when I first met the leaders of the new church. Would they understand

Edrie's condition? I needn't have worried. Like the people in our first church, they were kind and generous and gracious.

One of the most bitter-sweet experiences of our lives was the parting with our friends in Wiltshire. They had lived through the difficult years with us, and strong bonds of love held us together. I had thought that I would be there for the rest of my life, but instead God called me and I had to go.

On the last Sunday, I preached from Paul's parting words to the Ephesian elders: 'Now I commit you to God and to the word of his grace, which can build you up and give you an inheritance among all those who are sanctified' (Acts 20:32).

Luke tells us that, when Paul had finished speaking, he knelt down and prayed with them. They then wept as they parted.

Many tears were shed that last morning at church.

And so we began a new ministry. We had new challenges and great opportunities. We couldn't forget that Edrie was ill, but we refused to let it control or define us. All the time, we kept remembering to ask God to use our circumstances for his glory and not to waste our sorrows.

What are you praying for?

Long before Edrie became ill, we attended a large Christian conference. The main speaker talked about the importance of focused prayer. Often, our prayers are pretty vague: 'Please bless Mum and please bless Dad and please bless me.' It's so different from the great prayers of the Bible. The conference preacher was arguing for intelligence, imagination and effort in prayer.

To illustrate his point, he used a personal anecdote. At the start of his ministry, he had been pastoring a small church. In the congregation was a woman who was passing through a time of intense trial, suffering from a whole raft of serious ailments. At the same time, she was nursing a house-bound, terminally ill husband. It was nearly impossible for her to get to church, but one Sunday evening, thanks to the kindness of Christian friends, she had made it. When the pastor stood up to preach, his heart was warmed to see her sitting there in the back row. At the close of the service, it was obvious that she was anxious to get home quickly. He sprinted to the back and caught her just as she was leaving the building. He grasped her hand and thanked her for attending, assuring her that he was praying for her and her husband.

She stopped and looked quizzically into his eyes.

'Well thank you, pastor. Do you mind if I ask you a question? What are you praying for?'

He told us, his amused audience, 'My mind went blank. I mouthed a few banalities and felt very slightly embarrassed.'

Still holding his hand, the lady had smiled and spoken again.

'If you don't mind, can I tell you what to pray? Please pray that my husband and I don't waste this trial. Pray that God will help us to discern his purpose and be faithful in it.'

Life in Technicolor

Suffering can damage your focus or it can deepen our understanding. We can flitter it away in bitterness and regret, or we can ask God to help us to see and appreciate its value. We can waste it or we can benefit from it. Either way, as we saw earlier, the choice is ours.

During the days after Edrie and I had asked God to help us make our trials fruitful, I began to keep a journal. I wish I could say that I had kept this up – it would make the writing of this book so much easier! For almost six months, I wrote down my thoughts each day. What was God teaching us? What lessons did he want us to learn? How could we avoid wasting our suffering?

As I look back on those days, I believe that my relationship with God was closer than ever before. Do you remember *The Wizard of Oz*? Dorothy is transported from Kansas to the Land of Oz. In Kansas, everything is in black and white. In Oz, she suddenly discovers a world in Technicolor.

That was how I felt. Suddenly, things I knew seemed more vivid. The truths of the faith were more vibrant. The comforts of the faith were more intense. The love of God was more striking. The grace of God was more real. Suddenly, my Christian faith was in Technicolor.

So what did I write in my journal? What were the big lessons? Three stand out.

1. Suffering sweetens our fellowship with God

The first thing that happened was that my fellowship with God was deeper and more intense than it had ever been before.

Suffering is the best commentary on God's character, and pain is the finest exposition of his excellences. We discover more about God's grace when we come to the end of ourselves. You will never know that God is all you need, until God is all you have got.

In Philippians 3:10–11, Paul tells us his ambition:

> I want to know Christ – yes, to know the power of his resurrection and participation in his sufferings, becoming like him in his death, and so, somehow, attaining to the resurrection from the dead.

Paul already knows Christ, but he wants to know him better. This knowledge grows through the experience of the resurrection power of Christ released into his life through the ministry of the Holy Spirit. It also comes through sharing his sufferings. When we suffer as Christ did, we come to know Christ in a richer and fuller way.

Hudson Taylor, the great pioneer of Christian mission to Inland China, whom we met earlier, shared this truth with a group of young missionaries who were about to embark on a dangerous and costly life of missionary service:

> God will not lead you in a way that you would know, for that would profit you little. He will lead you in a way that you know not, so that through a thousand intimacies with himself the way may be forever memorable, both for you and for him.[1]

In those difficult days, there were some moments when time and eternity seemed to touch each other and God's presence was very real. They were some of the most memorable moments in my life. And they were ministered to me through pain.

'Nearer and clearer glimpses'

Many others would testify to the closeness of God in painful circumstances.

John Paton was a missionary who, with his young wife, went in 1858 to preach the gospel to the cannibals of the New Hebrides. He had been there for less than a year when his wife fell ill. In the absence of adequate medical attention, she died in his arms. Two weeks later, his baby son also sickened and died.

Paton felt crushed. The people to whom he was ministering suspected that the drought that was afflicting them had been caused by the missionary, and vowed to take his life. They stole his possessions and plotted to kill him. When an epidemic of measles killed a third of the people of Tanna, the town where Paton was working, his enemies surrounded the mission station. They burned the church, as well as Paton's meagre home. Paton had to hide up a tree. It was here that he had a sense of the grace and closeness of God:

> Never in all my sorrows did my Lord draw nearer to me and speak so soothingly to my soul. In the darkness, I cried to him and told him all my heart.

> I would have gone mad, but with my trembling hand I
> clasped the hand that was nailed to the cross for me and that
> now grips the sceptre of the universe.
>
> Peace and reassurance filled my soul. I had nearer and clearer
> glimpses of his face and the smile of my blessed Lord.[2]

As we have seen, these 'nearer and clearer glimpses' of Christ are not just for our personal benefit. God reveals himself to us so that we can be channels of his grace to others. In the end, we can only minister what God has ministered to us. Every day you will meet people who need to be encouraged in their Christian faith. The world is full of Christians who feel like giving up. One of the reasons why we suffer is so that we can know God better and, in so doing, point people to him.

In the end, we can only minister what God has ministered to us.

2. Suffering deepens our knowledge

A second lesson which I learned in those early days was that suffering deepens our love and understanding of truth. It not only gives us a unique and personal insight into the character of God, but it sharpens our understanding of the great truths of the faith that God has revealed in the Bible. Suffering focuses the mind wonderfully.

Suddenly, we find ourselves living in the pages of Scripture.

I have three gorgeous granddaughters. My oldest, the daughter of one of my sons, is called Esme. It has been a delight to see her parents teaching her the Bible and explaining that it is the Word of God and the most important book in the world.

In the height of summer, when the sun comes up at 4:30am, it is difficult to explain to a three-year-old that it is too early to get up. One morning, Esme's plaintive cries could be heard from her bedroom:

'Mummy, Daddy, the sun is shining. I want to get up.'

'It's too early, Esme. Go back to sleep.'

'I want a glass of water.'

'Go back to sleep.'

'I need the bathroom.'

'No, you don't. Go back to sleep.'

'I'm frightened.'

'No, you're not. Go back to sleep.'

With all avenues of appeal apparently exhausted, there was silence for a while. And then, triumphantly, one last unanswerable entreaty:

'Mummy, Daddy, please let me out. I've got to read the Bible. It's really important. It's the Word of God.'

Now, it's difficult to argue with that!

During my most difficult days, I came to love the Bible more than ever before. So did Edrie. When I arrived at the hospital, we would discuss what God had been showing us.

Delighting in the gospel

As I came to the Bible with a new passion and a new zeal, there was one thing that seemed to become more and more precious: indeed, I revelled in the glories of the Christian gospel. Paul could say that he was 'not ashamed' of the gospel, because it is the power of God (Romans 1:16–17). It is God's power at work in the world, changing lives and transforming communities. Evangelicals are 'gospel people'. We believe that the gospel must be defined biblically, experienced personally and communicated passionately. The gospel is the difference between life and death.

Suffering reminds us that everything in this world changes. And we want to anchor our lives in something that never changes. The eternal gospel of Jesus Christ is the anchor we need.

Sometimes, we forget how great it is to be a Christian. The gospel covers our past, present and future. We have been justified – God the righteous Judge has declared that we are righteous in his sight. We do not need to fear the judgment of the last day, because God has already passed his verdict and will never change his mind.

We are being sanctified: the Holy Spirit is making us holy. The process may be slow, and there may be many times when we feel disappointed at our own sinfulness and our stubborn resistance to his gentle-yet-persistent prompting. But he will not give up.

We will be glorified. One day, the process of salvation will be completed, and, in sinless bodies free from change and decay, we will see God. Never again will we suffer or sin. Never again will our lives be haunted by doubts or fears or anxieties.

As Christians, we look forward to a glorious inheritance that will never perish or spoil, never fade or disappoint. It is reserved in heaven for us, and we are kept by the power of God through faith until the day when we finally receive it. There is now no condemnation for those who are in Christ Jesus. God works all things for our good, and even the darkest providences have an ultimate purpose. We are more than conquerors through him who loved us, and we know that nothing will ever separate us from his love.

When we look back, there is no record of sin. When we look down, there is no hell to fear. When we look in, we find the peace of God, which passes all understanding, controlling our hearts and minds. When we look round, we see that God is working all things for our good. When we look onwards, we see that Christ is coming to take us home – heaven dawns for us like a glorious and long-expected new day. We are saved and sealed and satisfied and secure.

It's truly great to be a Christian!

All these blessings flow from the gospel. God the Father planned them for us in eternity. Christ purchased them for us when he died for us on the cross. The Holy Spirit has applied them all to us.

These are really great theological truths, and we rightly affirm and defend them. But it is suffering that seals them in our hearts. It is pain that drives us to a deeper understanding. It is anguish that strips away the insignificant fripperies that often control our thinking and drives us deep into the enjoyment of the great truths of the gospel of Jesus Christ.

I loved the gospel from the first moment that I felt its power and became a Christian. I have always loved the gospel. But I have never loved it as much as I have done since Edrie first became ill. Suffering has helped me to see deeper depths and higher heights, and to love God more. It has helped me to realize, as never before, just how wonderful it is to be a Christian.

3. Suffering humbles our hearts

The third lesson from those early days was that God uses suffering to keep us close to him. Back in 2 Corinthians 1, we find Paul explaining to the Corinthians why God had taken him into such a dark valley:

> We do not want you to be uninformed, brothers and sisters, about the troubles we experienced in the province of Asia. We were under great pressure, far beyond our ability to endure, so that we despaired of life itself. Indeed, we felt we had received the sentence of death. But this happened that we might not rely on ourselves but on God, who raises the dead.
> (2 Corinthians 1:8–9)

I hardly need to remind you that suffering undermines our self-reliance. It injects a healthy suspicion of our own gifts and wisdom and resources. I am not talking about some form of unwholesome negativity. But suffering drives us to our knees in the awareness that our own resources are inadequate. And it does not leave us there, but brings us to that place where we know that we have to trust God alone.

When doctors cannot help, and human wisdom reaches its final limit, and all our accumulated resources are spent, who else can we trust? The moment we get to that place, we are forced to cast ourselves into the arms of God. The experiences that Edrie has passed through have indeed been humiliating and crushing, but, frankly, amazingly liberating.

The thorn in the flesh

Such experiences defy human logic.

Paul returns to this at the end of 2 Corinthians where he talks about the 'thorn in my flesh' (2 Corinthians 12:1–10). He has been describing an experience of God that had transported him to the throne room of heaven (12:1–5). The danger with such experiences is that they feed our pride and inflate our egos. God's method of keeping him humble was to send 'a thorn in my flesh, a messenger of Satan, to torment me'. This was no minor inconvenience. Here was a serious problem, chronic and painful and humiliating. Theologians have imagined it in a variety of ways. Was it temptation (Calvin) or persecution (Luther)? Was it a medical condition: malaria or epilepsy or migraine or a chronic problem with his eyesight (Galatians 4:13–15)? We just don't know. Whatever it was, it seemed to threaten the effectiveness of Paul's ministry. He therefore asked God to take it away. In fact, he asked for this three times. But God said 'no'. Paul was asking the wrong question. Instead of asking for relief, he should have been asking for adequate grace to persevere and trust God. That was the reason for the thorn – God wanted Paul to discover the limitless resources of heaven. That reliance on God became the secret of the effectiveness of Paul's ministry.

Paul was asking the wrong question.

Listen to the words of the great Baptist preacher Charles Haddon Spurgeon:[3]

The other evening I was riding home after a heavy day's work. I felt very wearied, and sore depressed, when swiftly, and suddenly as a lightning flash, that text came to me, 'My grace is sufficient for thee.' I reached home and looked it up in the original, and at last it came to me in this way, 'MY grace is sufficient for thee'; and I said, 'I should think it is, Lord,' and burst out laughing. I never fully understood what the holy laughter of Abraham was until then. It seemed to make unbelief so absurd. It was as though some little fish, being very thirsty, was troubled about drinking the river dry, and Father Thames said, 'Drink away, little fish, my stream is sufficient for thee.' Or, it seemed after the seven years of plenty, a mouse feared it might die of famine; and Joseph might say, 'Cheer up, little mouse, my granaries are sufficient for thee.' Again, I imagined a man away up yonder, in a lofty mountain, saying to himself, 'I breathe so many cubic feet of air every year, I fear I shall exhaust the oxygen in the atmosphere,' but the earth might say, 'Breathe away, O man, and fill the lungs ever, my atmosphere is sufficient for thee.' Oh, brethren, be great believers! Little faith will bring your souls to Heaven, but great faith will bring Heaven to your souls.

There is a tremendously holy joy in resting in God.

So here is the big picture: don't waste your suffering.

Preaching what we know

When we arrived in Worcester, I was faced with the challenge of serving a new and vibrant church. After many years of sacrificial giving and courageous faith, the congregation of a small church in the centre of the ancient city had erected our magnificent building on a brand new housing estate. So while

'Woodgreen' was not really a new church, it felt like one. The people were wonderful and made us feel at home immediately. The church grew quickly and God smiled upon us. For the first three years, I worked as the only pastor, and I was stretched to the limit.

I quickly came to the conviction that the best way to serve the church was to be a man of prayer and preach God's Word in the power of the Holy Spirit. I was available for pastoral ministry and ran evangelistic courses quite regularly. I did the normal things that pastors are supposed to do, but I soon came to the conclusion that a church stands or falls on its prayer life and its preaching.

The first sermon I preached was from Exodus 15: Moses' great hymn of praise as he contemplated the deliverance through the Red Sea. The first series I preached was on the character of God.

I learned these great verities at the foot of the cross during days of trial and nights of pain.

Since then, I have preached many sermons. Edrie says that, if you were to put all my sermons end to end . . . they still would not reach a conclusion! Which is a little harsh really.

What have I preached? Well, the Bible of course! But, as I reflected on the emphasis of my ministry, it suddenly dawned on me that the sum and substance of my preaching has been the themes touched on in this chapter. Whenever I preach, I want people to know God better, to glory in the gospel of Jesus Christ and in him crucified. I want them to feel their own frailties, but to rejoice in Christ's utter sufficiency.

I learned these great verities at the foot of the cross during days of trial and nights of pain. Edrie and I have learned them together. They are the central themes of the Bible. They are what Christians need to know in order to reach maturity, what non-Christians need to know in order to be saved, what the church needs to know in order to be refreshed and revived and renewed.

We are to preach what we know and what we feel deeply. Suffering makes the truth more real than it has ever been before.

Do not waste your sorrows.

11. The love that will not let us go

After a number of years of wrestling with changed circumstances, Edrie and I settled into a routine of acceptance. Occasionally, though, I have been grieved that my beautiful wife has had to struggle with the simplest of tasks.

After a couple of embarrassing incidents, Edrie decided to give up driving. Getting used to using a wheelchair in public was tough. And going to parents' evenings at school and finding that some of the teachers spoke to me as if Edrie wasn't there was exceedingly galling. On shopping trips, I found myself becoming irrationally irate when able-bodied people pinched the limited number of disabled parking spaces. Edrie, on the other hand, would smile sweetly and tell me she was worried about my blood pressure.

You can learn to live with most things. But then Edrie's attacks started.

A new dimension of suffering

Edrie has never been diagnosed with MS, but, as I have said, the symptoms and prognosis of her condition seemed to be very similar. People would tell us that it was a tough call, but at least there is no pain with MS.[1] That had indeed been our experience. There had been a thousand indignities and humiliations, but Edrie had never been in pain. Then everything changed.

One day, Edrie complained about a tingling in her hands that was both annoying and painful. It faded after about an hour, and we thought nothing of it. Then it came back. This time the pain was more intense. Edrie described it as the sensation you have when you accidentally hold your hand in a fountain of steam. Worse still, it began to move up her arm and across her shoulders, and then reached her head. When that happened, she couldn't stand the light and had to bury her face in a pillow. I tried applying a hot-water bottle. I suggested painkillers. I prayed like mad. I felt totally hopeless.

After about an hour, Edrie recovered, and there seemed to be no after-effects. We went to bed exhausted, only for me to wake up in the middle of the night and find Edrie sitting on the side of the bed, shivering with pain. She was having another attack. She had a further one before breakfast, and so I made an emergency appointment to see the doctor. He was stumped and referred her to our neurologist.

Over the next fourteen months, the 'attacks' came to define our lives and became a dreaded daily reality. The neurologists tried a whole host of remedies. But nothing worked. They tested Edrie with as many as twenty different drugs. Some were not directly related to neurological conditions. The hope was that the side effects they produced might offer relief. Edrie attended a pain clinic. People prayed. But nothing worked.

During the attacks, Edrie would have to block out the light and she would groan with pain. They would usually last about an hour, reaching a terrible intensity after about twenty minutes and then trailing off. She was left exhausted and spent. On a good day, she might have five 'attacks'. One black day, I counted twelve. Edrie lost weight and lost hope. Pain brutalizes and degrades and dehumanizes.

I can remember so many incidents. Edrie and her sister took Keziah to Birmingham to see a performance of Tchaikovsky's *The Nutcracker*. It was a birthday treat for Kez, and she was so excited. But when the lights went down, Edrie suffered an attack. For the next three hours, several attacks arrived in rapid succession. For most of the performance, she sat with her head buried in her lap. Keziah was unable to enjoy her birthday treat as she anxiously rubbed her mum's back and told her that she didn't mind going home if that would help.

And then, as suddenly as the attacks had begun, they disappeared.

That was almost ten years ago. There have been moments when we feared they might be coming back, but there has been nothing to match those dark and desperate days.

People at church were great, and we were so grateful for numerous acts of kindness and compassion. But we almost went under. They were days when it always seemed to be winter and never Christmas. I felt torn apart with anxiety. I was totally helpless as I watched Edrie, so brave and courageous, weeping with pain and frustration. We felt abandoned.

What sustained us? I think the thing that kept us going was our reliance on God and a daily feeding of our faith with biblical truth. Many of the great lessons we have mentioned in previous chapters became even more real and precious during those black days. However, there was one truth that, for me, stood head and shoulders above the others. It was the fact of the love of God demonstrated in the sacrifice of his Son at Calvary. I lived in the Gospels, and particularly John's Gospel. I read it on my knees. I prayed it. I preached it. As I did these things, Jesus became more and more precious to me. Looking at his love and the suffering he experienced for me helped me to look beyond the apparent meaninglessness of our suffering to see that, at the heart of the Godhead, is a Saviour who knows and feels and sympathizes with our suffering.

An open secret

John's Gospel gives us a sublime and peerless account of the life of Jesus. John begins with an open secret: Jesus Christ is both fully divine and fully human. In the prologue (John 1:1–18), he tells us three things about Jesus.

1. Jesus is God

Firstly, he is God:

> In the beginning was the Word, and the Word was with God, and the Word was God. He was with God in the beginning. Through him all things were made; without him nothing was made that has been made. In him was life, and that life was the light of all mankind. The light shines in the darkness, and the darkness has not overcome it.
> (John 1:1–5)

John affirms Jesus' eternity ('in the beginning'), his personality ('with God') and his deity ('was God'). The proof of his deity is that he can do things that only God can do. This includes creation ('through him all things were made'), animation ('in him was life') and revelation ('that life was the light of all mankind'). The rest of the Gospel will demonstrate and substantiate these truths.

When I was a kid, I often stayed with my granny. If we were due for a walk and it was raining, she would send me to check it out. She wanted to know if it was 'wet rain'. What she was asking was whether it was just a brief drizzle or the kind of rain that, if you braved it, would leave you drenched to the skin. When we walk through the pages of John's Gospel, we are drenched to the skin with the revelation of Christ's full and perfect deity. It's not a drizzle; it's a downpour. He is 'co-equal and co-eternal' with the Father. His claims are undeniable, his miracles are irrefutable and his deity is incontestable. The Gospel reaches its climax in

Thomas's confession: 'My Lord and my God' (John 20:28). The confession of his deity is not a matter of academic theological interest; it is a matter of life and death (20:31).

2. The Word became flesh

Secondly, John also affirms Jesus' full humanity:

> The Word became flesh and made his dwelling among us. We have seen his glory, the glory of the one and only Son, who came from the Father, full of grace and truth.
> (1:14)

When we meet Jesus, we meet a real man. The eternal Word became 'flesh'. Jesus did not merely appear human; he took humanity to himself. It was not an illusion or an elaborate hoax. He was truly and fully human – a real man among real men. Again, this is clearly affirmed in the rest of the Gospel. It is John who tells us that Jesus was tired (4:6) and thirsty (4:7); that he wept with grief and frustration (11:35); that he bled blood and water from his pierced side (19:34).

In my darkest days, days when the 'attacks' were at their height, I would be comforted by the truth of the genuine humanity and sympathy of Christ. At the heart of deity is a Saviour who knows our broken hearts and feels for our sorrows:

> Before the throne of God above
> I have a strong and perfect plea.
> A great High Priest whose Name is Love
> Who ever lives and pleads for me.
> My name is graven on His hands,
> My name is written on His heart.
> I know that while in heav'n He stands
> No tongue can bid me thence depart.[2]

His love for me was planned in eternity, but forged amid the pains of living in a fallen world. God is not a distant and indifferent deity, not a kind of Buddha looking at a suffering world through the eyes of cool unconcerned detachment, but my great High Priest whose name is love. When Edrie wept in the darkness and I wept with her, the Saviour was near, carrying us both on his heart and presenting us to his Father.

The early Church Fathers adored this truth and struggled to give some account of how Jesus could be fully God and fully man at the same time. They concluded that he was one person with two distinct natures. When the Word became flesh, he did not cease to be God, but took a real human nature to himself. He never abandoned his humanity when he returned to heaven. In a real sense, the dust of the earth is on the throne of the universe. How do the two natures relate? The Fathers wanted to affirm this mystery, and said that the Son's divine nature was permanently united to a human nature, without confusion, change, division or separation.

I love the doctrine of the incarnation. I love the fact that it is true; I love the fact that it is mysterious and awesome; I love the fact that it assures me that Christ knows and understands my deepest distresses.

3. God rolled up his sleeves

Thirdly, John affirms that Jesus is here:

> No one has ever seen God, but the one and only Son, who is himself God and is in the closest relationship with the Father, has made him known.
> (1:18)

In the person of Jesus Christ, God steps into the pages of history and fully reveals himself to us. In the past, God may have spoken through his servants, the prophets, but, in these last days, he has spoken to us by his Son (Hebrews 1:1–4). This is the full and final revelation. Nothing compares to this. To know the Son is to know the Father. To love the Son is to love the Father. To obey the Son is to obey the Father and to hate the Son is to hate the Father.

The whole Gospel of John is intended to be a revelation of the character of God. It reveals his purity and power, his wisdom and holiness. But most of all, it reveals his love:

> For God so loved the world that he gave his one and only Son,
> that whoever believes in him shall not perish but have eternal life.
> (3:16)

God loves us more than we can imagine and he wants us to know it. If we wish to see and feel and be astounded by this staggering love, then John's Gospel is a good place to begin.

A book in two parts

After his prologue, John's Gospel falls into two parts. The first describes the three years of Jesus' ministry. It has been called the 'Book of Signs' (John 1:19 – 11:57). John records seven miracles or signs that testify to the nature of Jesus' mission and the truth of his deity.

However, the underlying motif is the certainty of his death. From the beginning of his ministry, Jesus knows that he has come to die (2:18–22; 3:14–16). As the Good Shepherd, he proves his love for the sheep by laying down his life for them (10:11, 14, 17–18). The first half of the Gospel ends with the plot to kill him (11:45–57).

The second half of John has been described as the 'Book of Suffering' (12:1 – 21:25). It is stunning. After setting the scene (12:1–50), John then spends seven chapters describing the last twenty-four hours of the earthly life of Jesus, leading up to his crucifixion, death and burial (13:1 – 19:42). It is clear that the cross is absolutely central to the life of Jesus and to John's portrayal of it. The Gospel ends with the affirmation of the resurrection of Jesus (20:1 – 21:25), a real, historical and datable event.

In the shadow of the cross

The life of Jesus is the supreme source of comfort for the suffering Christian. It demonstrates his love for us. His incarnation is the proof that he knows and feels our pain. His teaching is a guide in the darkness. His pastoral care demonstrates his compassion. His resurrection proves that death will not have the final word. It also proves that, even though suffering may appear meaningless, God has deep and mysterious purposes,

The life of Jesus is the supreme source of comfort for the suffering Christian.

which will one day make sense of it. His triumph over all the enemies of humanity is a reminder that God will bring about a new heaven and a new earth. His ascension proves that he is in heaven watching over us, praying for us and preparing a place for us. His return is the great hope that one day our suffering will end forever.

The wondrous cross

I found that it was thinking about the cross that became the greatest comfort in those dark days.

Come with me to John 12, the porch that leads into the palace of Jesus' suffering. Jesus has been anointed at Bethany, a prophetic action pointing ahead to his death (12:1–11). He has then ridden in triumph into the city of Jerusalem (12:12–19). It is at this point that 'some Greeks among those who went up to worship at the festival' come to seek an audience with Jesus (John 12:20–22). This acts as a kind of trigger for Jesus, and he begins to speak about the cross and its meaning to him:

> Jesus replied, 'The hour has come for the Son of Man to be glorified. Very truly I tell you, unless a grain of wheat falls to the ground and dies, it remains only a single seed. But if it dies, it produces many seeds. Anyone who loves their life will lose it, while anyone who hates their life in this world will keep it for eternal life. Whoever serves me must follow me; and where I am, my servant also will be. My Father will honour the one who serves me.
>
> 'Now my soul is troubled, and what shall I say? "Father, save me from this hour"? No, it was for this very reason I came to this hour. Father, glorify your name!'
>
> Then a voice came from heaven, 'I have glorified it, and will glorify it again.' The crowd that was there and heard it said it had thundered; others said an angel had spoken to him.
>
> Jesus said, 'This voice was for your benefit, not mine. Now is the time for judgment on this world; now the prince of this world will be driven out. And I, when I am lifted up from the earth, will draw all people to myself.' He said this to show the kind of death he was going to die.
> (John 12:23–33)

Here is a unique insight into Jesus' own understanding of the purpose of his crucifixion. He tells us five things about the cross.

1. Glory

Firstly, it was a place of glory (verses 23, 28). When we think of God's glory, we usually think about his awe-inspiring wonder, breath-taking splendour and spine-tingling majesty. We think of the greatness of his creation or the power of his miracles or the moments when he appears to people, and they are left over-whelmed and stunned.

We do not think of the cross. At the cross, Jesus is beaten so that he can barely stand, stripped of his clothes, thrown to the ground, hammered to a piece of wood and lifted up between heaven and earth. For the people of his day, crucifixion was a scandal and a shame, a dirty word never to be mentioned in polite society. It was only fit for slaves and the lowest, most depraved criminals.

Yet Jesus describes it as the place where he will be glorified. In his shame and rejection, he will reveal the glory of God as never before. God will declare his love and display his holiness and demonstrate his power and define his wisdom on an unprecedented scale. Indeed, Paul will later say that he has come to boast in the cross (Galatians 6:14).

Edrie and I came to boast in the cross, to see that the pain we were going through was an opportunity to show that, in spite of our suffering, we could still trust God and bring him glory. Some people are called to preach great sermons to the glory of God, and others are called to mend cars or teach children or heal bodies to the glory of God. We were called to suffer for the glory of God.

The main question we needed to ask was not 'why?' but 'how?'. How can we bring glory to Christ in the midst of a series of 'attacks' which have all but robbed us of the day? How do we show our kids, who cannot understand what is happening to Mum, that we still love and trust God and believe he knows best? How do I glorify God in my preaching and pastoring when I have been up half the night struggling with the darkness?

If the cross can be a place of glory, so too can our deepest distresses.

2. Fruit

Secondly, the cross was a place of fruitfulness (24–26). Jesus reminds us of what all farmers know. If seeds are to bear fruit, they must be laid in the ground so that they can die. A stored and protected seed is fruitless. One laid out to die bears a harvest of fruit.

From this simple principle, Jesus is teaching that his death is the inevitable condition of the successfulness of his mission. Down through the ages, people have portrayed Jesus in a number of guises: teacher, rabbi, miracle-worker, social reformer, philosopher, celestial celebrity. However we define his ministry, it is clear that, at the centre of Jesus' own understanding, is the necessity of the cross. If he had come to earth, healed crowds, revealed that he was God in the flesh, preached sublime sermons and then returned to heaven without dying, his mission would have been a failure. His death was the condition of the salvation of the world. He could not '[bring] many sons and daughters to glory' unless he died first (Hebrews 2:10–18).

And the principle applies to us too (12:25–26). God wants us to be fruitful. One of the conditions is a willingness to die to self – to our own comforts and dreams and expectations – and to follow Jesus into the ground. Sowing means death and darkness and loneliness. Only as we die to self can we bear much fruit.

Edrie's and my experience felt like a kind of dying. What we had expected as a young married couple hadn't worked out. But we came to see many times over that our suffering was God's method of fruitfulness. The cross of Jesus became our inspiration, our model and our encouragement in ministry.

3. Horror

Thirdly, the cross was a place of horror. Verse 27 gives us a unique window into the soul of Jesus as he faced the cross: 'Now my soul is troubled, and what shall I say? "Father, save me from this hour"?'

The word 'troubled' carries the idea of being perplexed and agitated and amazed. It can be used of a tempestuous storm at sea. The waves rise and threaten to sink our poor, pathetic little boat. Light has gone, and deepest darkest surrounds us. That is the word Jesus uses to describe his inner turmoil. We are reminded of the Garden of Gethsemane where he was also 'sorrowful and troubled', confessing that his soul was overwhelmed with sorrow to the point of death (Matthew 26:37–38). There, he pleaded for the cup of suffering to be taken away (Mark 14:36), and his sweat was like great drops of blood (Luke 22:44).

What caused Jesus such horror? The physical pain and the shame of crucifixion certainly. But it was more than that. Jesus died as a substitute and, in his death, satisfied the Father's just and holy wrath against our sin. Like a lightening conductor, he drew to himself the entire wrath that his people deserved. God treated his Son as if he were the worst sinner to walk on the face of the earth. During the three hours of darkness, he who knew no sin was made sin for us. During his earthly ministry, Jesus always spoke of God as his Father, often using the intimate name 'Abba, Father'. He lived in the consciousness of God's smile. But, as he bears our sins and faces his Father's wrath, out of the darkness, he cries, 'My God, my God, why have you forsaken me?' This alone explains the horror of anticipation with which he approaches the cross.

This comforted me, because I knew that his suffering – on a greater scale than anything any human being can ever go through – was for me. His death had freed me from hell – the ultimate horror in God's universe. He was forsaken so that I never would be. He tasted hell so that I never would do. That helped to get our suffering into perspective.

But there was more than that: these words gave us permission to be human! Jesus was the perfect man. He is primarily our Saviour, but, once we have trusted him, he is also our model. He approached suffering with honesty and integrity. He was not glib or casual about what he was about to face – in fact, it filled him with horror. In the garden, there was real apprehension; on the cross, there was real agony. I look at Jesus and, in a small way, feel something of the fellowship of his suffering.

4. Mission

Fourthly, the cross was a place of destiny (27–28). As Jesus approached, it was with deep apprehension, but also sublime submission:

> Now my soul is troubled, and what shall I say? 'Father, save me from this hour'? No, it was for this very reason I came to this hour. Father, glorify your name!
> (John 12:27–28)

Jesus saw the cross as his hour of destiny, the moment for which he had been born. Jesus was not a 'good man who died tragically young', but the eternal Son of God who left the glory of heaven to fulfil the mission that the Father had given him. From the start, he was the 'Lamb of God, who takes away the sin of the world' (John 1:29), conscious that he was operating according to a divine timetable, waiting for 'the hour' which the Father had set. Later, as he approaches this final moment of destiny, he prays to his Father and reminds him of the glory they shared before the foundation of the earth (John 17:1–5). In his first sermon, Peter tells his hearers that Jesus' death was not a lapse of judgment or an unexpected turn of events. Human beings bore responsibility for their sinful actions, but it all happened because it was part of God's predetermined plan (Acts 2:22–24).

And what was the Father's response?

> Then a voice came from heaven, 'I have glorified it, and will glorify it again.'
> (John 12:28)

The Father acknowledges the Son's submission, confirms him in his obedience and promises his support.

How does this help us? Because it proves that even the darkest providences are part of God's plan and purpose for his people. God has an eternal plan, and it will not fail. If something as horrific as the cross falls within the orbit of God's purposes, then so too do our trials and heartbreaks. The cross was not 'plan B', nor were the attacks that disrupted our lives.

5. Victory

Finally, the cross was a place of victory (31–32):

> Now is the time for judgment on this world; now the prince of this world will be driven out. And I, when I am lifted up from the earth, will draw all people to myself.
> (John 12:31–32)

The cross looked like the place of ultimate defeat. Satan had triumphed, death was victorious, the mission of Jesus had failed and the plans of God had been frustrated. In fact, it was the place of ultimate triumph. Through his death on the cross, Jesus crushed Satan's head (Genesis 3:15) and pulled him down from his pretended throne. He disarmed the devil once and for all (Colossians 2:13–15) and removed the sting of death (1 Corinthians 15:50–56). It is through the preaching of the cross that the mission of the church was launched in the world, resulting in the salvation of all kinds of people (Matthew 28:18–20; 1 Corinthians 2:1–5).

Even our apparent defeats can be turned into victories by the grace and power of God. The cross shows what God can achieve through pain – what he can bring about when his children willingly submit to him.

Martin Luther once said that all our theology has to be done within earshot of Calvary.[3] All our suffering needs to be done there too. As we gaze at the cross, God is able to 'sanctify to us our deepest distress'.[4]

O love that will not let me go

When he was twenty years old, the poet and preacher George Matheson discovered that he was going blind. When he told his fiancée, she responded that she could not marry a blind man and so broke off the engagement. His sister cared for him. But in 1882, she got married. On the evening before the wedding, sitting alone and thinking about the prospect of living alone, he was filled with grief. He probably remembered his own lost love. It was out of this sense of profound loneliness and spiritual darkness that he wrote a hymn encouraging us to look at our sufferings through the lens of God's love poured out for us on Calvary:

> O Love that will not let me go,
> I rest my weary soul in thee;
> I give thee back the life I owe,
> That in thine ocean depths its flow
> May richer, fuller be.
>
> O light that follows all my way,
> I yield my flickering torch to thee;
> My heart restores its borrowed ray,
> That in thy sunshine's blaze its day
> May brighter, fairer be.
>
> O Joy that seekest me through pain,
> I cannot close my heart to thee;
> I trace the rainbow through the rain,
> And feel the promise is not vain,
> That morn shall tearless be.

O Cross that lifts up my head,
I dare not ask to fly from thee;
I lay in dust life's glory dead,
And from the ground there blossoms red
Life that shall endless be.[5]

Pain is for a moment. The life Jesus offers is endless.

12. Living in hope

Recently, I took Edrie to hospital.

Eight months before, she had had a nasty fall – her balance never returned after the original onset of her illness. She falls over perhaps once a month on average. This time, she had badly bruised her right hand. This was quite significant, because she needed both hands to use her wheelchair. We went to a doctor who told us that it was sprained rather than broken. When it did not improve after a month, Edrie went for physio-therapy. That continued throughout the summer. Still there was no improvement. She experienced excruciating pain in her hand and, as a result, increasing weakness. She found it almost impossible to hold a cup of coffee. So she was referred to a specialist.

The guy was great. After an X-ray, he spent half an hour holding my wife's hand – that's what you get to do when you are an expert on hands and wrists. He told her that, when she had fallen, she had damaged a ligament which meant that the bones in the hand were now misaligned. Two of the bones were rubbing, causing the pain. He could fuse them together, but that would result in a loss of movement. A better solution would be to remove some of the pain receptors so that Edrie could no longer feel the pain. To show us what it would be like, he injected the area with a strong anaesthetic. By the time we got home, it was working. Edrie smiled with triumph as she lifted a cup of coffee for the first time in months.

At the time of writing, we are going ahead with the operation, if our 'handyman' still thinks it advisable.

Will it never end?

Why do I tell you this story?

Partly because it brings us up to date, but also partly because it illustrates the constant deterioration that Edrie's body is experiencing. We often wonder if anything else could possibly go wrong – and then it does. 'I feel like an old crock sometimes,' Edrie tells me.

We were at a conference a few months ago, and a couple came across to us. They were surprised to see us. The lady was genuinely pleased to see Edrie:

'How lovely it is to see you after all these years. You look so well. I honestly expected that the Lord would have taken you to heaven by now!'

As we reflected on it afterwards, Edrie said that the worst part about it was that she felt exactly the same.

'How long can this go on? Will it never end?' we ask.

One time, we were sitting in our local park. A group of runners jogged by. They looked pretty serious; maybe they were training for the Birmingham half-marathon. Among their number were a couple of guys who looked as if they were in their late sixties. They sped by without any apparent mobility problems. Edrie, by contrast, has not walked unaided for twenty years. She used to love to dance to the music of a popular contemporary quartet called ABBA. She has not been able to cross the living room without fear of falling for a long time

– sometimes I have found her crawling on her hands and knees because of the danger of taking a tumble. Our kids cannot remember the last time they saw their mum running – Emmaus has never even seen her walk unaided.

Coping is a daily challenge. So how do we manage? We both cultivate our sense of humour; we try to smile at the situation and to see the funny side every time. We rely on God's promises and live by the truths articulated in this book.

But, more than that, we live in hope.

Hope – the poor relation

Paul identifies the trio of Christian virtues as faith, hope and love (1 Corinthians 13:13). Faith and love have a pretty good press. We know that we are saved by faith and we are called to walk by faith. We admire the heroes of the faith in the Bible. We realize that the Bible's promises and blessings are accessed by faith. The Bible tells us that, without faith, we cannot please God. So faith is pretty important.

The same is true of love. God is love and he loves us. The commandments are summarized by the command to love God with all our heart and soul and strength and mind and to love our neighbour as ourselves. If we lack love, then our ministry is worthless and we need to make sure that we do not lose our first love. So love is pretty important too.

But what about hope? When was the last time you heard a sermon on the subject of hope? Have you ever heard a Christian say that it is impossible to live for Christ if you do not live in hope? Who were the great men and women of hope in the Bible? It is easy for hope to feel like a bit of a poor relation. We give it lip service, but it doesn't really figure very much in our thinking.

For Edrie and me, hope has been a vital ingredient. We have seen countless doctors. We have been reassured by numerous well-meaning Christians that they are convinced that God is going to heal Edrie. And we have reached the conclusion that Edrie will never recover in this life. We have come to see that it is tough living in the middle of the book and that, the older you get, the tougher it becomes. And as these things have dawned on us, we have discovered the power of hope.

In the Bible, hope is not a vague expectation – a kind of fingers-crossed wishful thinking. Rather, it is the Bible's shorthand for unconditional certainty. Hope is a sure and confident expectation about the future, based on a trust in God's sovereignty and a confidence in his faithfulness. True hope is future-orientated and grounded in the character of God and the fact that he has committed himself to us in the form of his unbreakable promises. Hope is therefore the confident anticipation of a future outcome.

True hope is future-orientated and grounded in the character of God.

Beyond the middle of the book

The New Testament is a book of unfinished business. Christ's return is its central heartbeat. It is the 'blessed hope' of the church that helps it to endure fire and sword and suffering.

The last book in the Bible is the Revelation of John. It is designed to comfort persecuted Christians. It contains a promise that is repeated three times:

> Look, I am coming soon! Blessed is the one who keeps the words of the prophecy written in this scroll.
> (Revelation 22:7)

And again:

> Look, I am coming soon! My reward is with me, and I will give to
> each person according to what they have done. I am the Alpha and
> the Omega, the First and the Last, the Beginning and the End.
> (Revelation 22:12–13)

And again:

> He who testifies to these things says, 'Yes, I am coming soon.'
> Amen. Come, Lord Jesus.
> The grace of the Lord Jesus be with God's people. Amen.
> (Revelation 22:20–21)

The return of Jesus is certain.

In a tantalizing vision of the future, the apostle John describes
the contents of the future hope in Revelation 21:1 – 22:6. Here
his focus is on the 'new heaven and the new earth'.

John's final picture is in three frames.

1. A renewed cosmos

The first frame reveals a renewed cosmos (21:1–8).

In sublime and moving words, John opens his vision by
describing a new heaven and a new earth (21:1). He deliberately
uses the language of Genesis 1:1 to remind us of the first
creation. Right now, this world is fallen and broken. It longs for
renewal. And God will miraculously restore it.

As he gazes at this new creation, John sees a beautiful new
city descending from heaven (21:2). In highly symbolic language,
we are assured of the final victory of the city of God over all the
cities of this world. This city symbolizes the final destiny of
the church. She is the stunningly gorgeous bride of Christ who
will reign with him forever on a renewed earth.

But what is the central attraction of this city?

And I heard a loud voice from the throne saying, 'Look! God's dwelling-place is now among the people, and he will dwell with them. They will be his people, and God himself will be with them and be their God.
(Revelation 21:3)

God will be present with his people as he was in the garden of Eden. We will walk in intimate and eternal fellowship with him. This is the heart of our hope, the supreme goal of humanity and the reason for which God created us. In this new world, we will experience a new quality and condition of life, purged of all the consequences of the curse (21:4). At the heart of this will be the vision of God.

This first frame closes with the assurance that these things will certainly happen (21:5–6), except for those who remain unforgiven (21:8).

Here is our hope. The world is damaged and broken, but it will be restored.

In 1974, a vandal broke into King's College Chapel in Cambridge. He scrawled graffiti across the canvas of Peter Paul Rubens' famous painting *The Adoration of the Magi*. For a few days, the art establishment held its breath. Was the irreplaceable creation ruined? An expert in the restoration of canvases was called to examine the painting. Finally came the announcement: 'The masterpiece is damaged, but it can be fully restored.'

The masterpiece is damaged, but it can be fully restored.

We live in a cosmos that is damaged, but that's not the end: one day it will be fully restored. Sin has scarred the whole creation and damaged the very fabric of this world. It should not surprise us when things go wrong – decay inhabits our DNA, and it is only a matter of time before we come to experience the reality of the human condition. But do not despair. A new world is coming where rot and ruin are banished forever. The masterpiece is damaged, but it can be fully restored.

2. A radiant city

The second frame (Revelation 21:9–27) describes the radiant city introduced in the second verse. John does this using a wonderful riot of symbols. Most of these graphic images are drawn directly from the Old Testament. Although they are designed to fire our imagination and kindle our hope, we must not forget that they point to concrete realities.

Look at the picture John paints of this magnificent city and allow it to inspire you. Think about its origin (21:9–11). It comes down from heaven. It is God's gift, not man's achievement. We should labour to alleviate the sufferings of this world, but we need to remember that the curse will not be removed until Christ returns. Emperors and potentates have attempted to establish kingdoms that will last forever, but they all end in dust. We await the eternal kingdom, which only King Jesus can establish.

Consider its walls and its foundations (21:12–14). In the ancient world, the security of a city depended on the strength of its walls. This heavenly city is a place of maximum security. All evil is excluded forever. The gates are inscribed with the names of the twelve patriarchs, and on the foundations we find the names of the twelve apostles. Clearly, they are meant to represent the presence of both Old and New Testament saints. The community of heaven consists of all the people of God down the ages of history: Abraham, Moses, David and the prophets; Matthew, Mark, Luke and John; Augustine, Luther, Calvin and my dad!

Reflect on its dimensions (21:15–17). It is enormous; a cube of 12,000 stadia has sides that are almost 1,400 miles.[1] Symbolic, yes, but it is meant to indicate a vastness of scale that is almost unimaginable. It prepares us for the fact that this city is full of so many people from every tribe and tongue and nation that no-one will be able to compute the number.

Ponder its beauty (verses 18–21). Gold is commonplace in this heavenly city, which is adorned with every type of precious stone and whose twelve gates are each a massive pearl. Again, we must remember that we are dealing with symbols, but they are meant to whet our appetite: a beautiful city for a redeemed people. We cannot imagine the glories of the final state.

Wonder at its glory (verses 22–27). Just as the climax of the first frame is the presence of God with his people, so the glory of the city is that God dwells at its centre:

> I did not see a temple in the city, because the Lord God
> Almighty and the Lamb are its temple. The city does not need
> the sun or the moon to shine on it, for the glory of God gives it
> light, and the Lamb is its lamp. The nations will walk by its light,
> and the kings of the earth will bring their splendour into it.
> (Revelation 21:22–24)

Nothing could be more glorious than this. We have been created for this very thing: to know God and live in close fellowship with our Creator. If death is existence without God, then life is existence in fellowship with God, and eternal life is an eternal and intimate relationship with the Lord and the Lamb.

3. A restored garden

The final frame is of a restored garden, and this is the most astonishing image of all:

> Then the angel showed me the river of the water of life, as clear
> as crystal, flowing from the throne of God and of the Lamb

down the middle of the great street of the city. On each side of the river stood the tree of life, bearing twelve crops of fruit, yielding its fruit every month. And the leaves of the tree are for the healing of the nations. No longer will there be any curse. The throne of God and of the Lamb will be in the city, and his servants will serve him. They will see his face, and his name will be on their foreheads. There will be no more night. They will not need the light of a lamp or the light of the sun, for the Lord God will give them light. And they will reign for ever and ever. (Revelation 22:1–5)

In a world where there is no curse, separation from God will be a thing of the past. Exile was the ultimate judgment for those who rebelled against God; Adam was exiled from Eden; Israel was exiled from the Promised Land; on the cross, Christ was exiled from the gracious presence of his Father. Because of the death of Christ, we have been reconciled to God. However, there is a real sense in which we are still living in exile – still strangers and pilgrims. But our great hope is that one day the exile will be over and we will be home, dwelling forever in God's presence.

At present, we cannot see God face to face and survive (Exodus 33:20), but in heaven this will be a genuine experience (22:4). This vision of God is the ultimate goal of human existence.

One day, paradise will be restored. As we examine the bookends of the Bible, we discover a number of clear parallels between Genesis 1 – 3 and Revelation 21 – 22. However, as we scrutinize the details, we see that the new creation is superior to the old one.

Eden is marked by day and night (Genesis 1:5); in heaven, there is no night (Revelation 21:5). In Eden, the curse is pronounced (Genesis 3:14–19); in heaven, the curse is removed (Revelation 22:3). In Eden, death can enter in (Genesis 3:19); in heaven, death is removed forever (Revelation 21:4). The door is shut on Eden (Genesis 3:24); in heaven, the doors are thrown open forever (Revelation 21:5). In Eden, access to the tree of life is denied (Genesis 3:24); in heaven, there is ready and open access (Revelation 21:25).

The new creation will last 'for ever and ever' (Revelation 22:5). There will be no sea, hence no chaos to disrupt order (Revelation 21:1). Nothing impure will be permitted to enter in (Revelation 21:27). Satan will not be present to deceive and tempt us into sin (Revelation 20:10). And there will be no possibility of a further fall in the new creation.

When God keeps us waiting

Hope is faith in the future dimension, trusting in God even when he keeps you waiting.

I have told you about my dad. Let me now tell you about my mum. The kindest and most generous woman I have ever met, like Dad, she never put any stumbling block in the way of my faith. But she was not interested in my Christianity. While Dad grew warmer to it, Mum grew cooler. When Dad was saved and started attending church, she felt a little left out, but this did nothing to attract her to her husband's new faith.

Then Dad died. Mum was not bitter, but I know she prayed about it and her prayers were 'unanswered'.

She lived a few doors away from the little church where Edrie and I had first met. My dad's funeral took place there. Afterwards, Mum was adamant that she would never attend again – and for over twenty years she didn't.

When Edrie became ill, Mum asked questions, but was wonderfully supportive. We occasionally talked about our faith, but she really didn't want to know:

'I don't understand. You are only trying to do good things and help people. Why would God do this to you?'

For forty years, I prayed for her every day. When we got married, Edrie joined me in prayer. I longed for my mum to come to know Jesus as I did. The children all adored 'Nanny' and prayed for her as well.

Out of the blue, my son rang me one day to tell me that Julie, my sister, wanted to find out how to become a Christian. She was saved and baptized and became a member of that same little church.

But still Mum held out. Then she fell ill – very ill. Mum had beaten cancer, but now her heart seemed to be failing. My sister, who was nursing her, rang to tell me that the doctor had indicated that the situation was grave.

It was a Monday morning. I had attended a prayer meeting early every Monday morning for over ten years. When you pray with the same people for such a long time, you feel able to share your heart with them. That's what I did that Monday. Through my tears, I asked for prayer:

'I am going to see my mum. I don't know how long she has. I long to be able to share the gospel with her. If she doesn't want to know, I think I'll die.'

We prayed passionately that morning. I set off for Birmingham, a journey of about thirty miles. I found myself stopping a couple of times just to cry to God, aware that this might be the last chance my mum would have to become a Christian.

When I arrived, she looked so small and frail lying in the big bed with its crisp white sheets. She recognized me and smiled. I held her hand. We sat for a while, and I told her I loved her. Then, praying under my breath, I asked God to give me the words to speak.

'Mum, do you know where Dad is?'

'Yes. He's in heaven, isn't he?'

'Yes, Mum. Do you know how he got there?'

'No.'

'Would you like me to tell you?'

In the past, she would simply have said she was not interested. She seemed to take forever to reply. Then:

'Yes, please. I think I would.'

So I told her about the Saviour of sinners. I told her about the dying thief who came to Jesus at the end of his life. I told her that we are not saved by our good deeds but by faith in Christ alone. I told her what Dad had believed and how he had come to trust in Jesus.

When I had finished, she looked quite pensive for a while and then she said, 'Do you think that I could become a Christian?'

Could she?

Of course she could!

Sitting with my mum's hand in mine, I led her to Christ. The angels in heaven rejoiced – but nothing like the joy in my own heart. Edrie had been praying at home, and, when I told her, she didn't believe me!

And then God did something amazing – he spared my mum's life. She slowly recovered. She is still very frail and weak, but she returned to a measure of health.

And the first thing she did when she was able? She went to the church she had vowed she would never attend, the church where I had first met Edrie, where my dad had learned to love Jesus, where my sister was now an enthusiastic member. She came to the Lord and she came to church. I was there on the first Sunday that Mum received bread and wine at the Lord's Table (communion). She looked down the row to where I was sitting and smiled at me with the most seraphic smile I have ever seen. And then, just before she took the bread for the first time, she raised her hand and gave me a thumbs-up.

I have studied theology for over thirty-five years. I have delved into systematics and linguistics. I have wrestled with biblical theology and historical theology. I have sailed on seas of deep and glorious theological reflection. But sitting at the back of that little church, I have to say that that thumbs-up was the most profound theological symbol I had ever seen.

In answer to the prayers of over forty years, prayers from the lips of most of the people who loved her, God had used suffering to break into my mum's life. He had broken down her barriers and won her heart with his tender love. And one day, she will join my dad in heaven.

Dancing to the music of eternity

Edrie always loved dancing. Being unable to dance is not her greatest trial, but it grieves her that she will never be able to do this again in this world. We no longer go to church barn dances – they are just too painful. It is tough to be reminded of what you have lost.

However, we have an 'arrangement'. When we get to heaven, we are going to seek each other out. Will we know each other? I'm pretty certain that we will. And then, I will take my beautiful wife in my arms, and we will dance together as we are over- whelmed with gratitude to God for his grace in bringing us into the glory of the new creation. We will dance to the sounds of the music of eternity. It will be quite an amazing experience, since I have never danced with anyone in my life, anywhere or at any time. But when we get to heaven, we will get to do a lot of things we have never done before!

By the seaside in Savannah

Well, I have to confess I'm not too sure about the dancing, but I do know that the best is yet to be.

A few years ago, I was at a conference in Savannah in Georgia on the Eastern seaboard of the USA. During a free afternoon, we went down to the sea. Before me was the Atlantic Ocean. Three thousand miles to the east is continental Europe. The same ocean that lapped at my feet touches the British coast. The Atlantic is something like 5,000 miles from north to south. In places, it is a mile deep. It is the second largest ocean in the world. It covers a total area of over 41 million square miles, approximately a fifth of the earth's surface.[2] It must contain billions and billions of gallons of water.

As I stood on the shore, I stooped and filled the palm of my hand with seawater. Here is my question: did I hold the Atlantic in the palm of my hand?

The answer is both 'yes' and 'no'. Of course, I did not hold the whole ocean in my hand. In no way could the slight dampness on my palm be equated with the whole ocean. And yet, I was holding authentic Atlantic Ocean. If I had bottled it and taken it home, I would have been carrying genuine Atlantic Ocean through customs.

During this life, we have a genuine experience of God. Our relationship is supposed to deepen and grow over the years. Suffering and trials are often the means that God sends. The Lord is never as precious as when suffering drives us into his arms. And yet, our knowledge now is nothing compared to the fullness of knowledge we will come to experience in eternity. Like the dampness on my hand compared to the vastness of the Atlantic, so our present experience is tiny compared with the knowledge to come. For eternity, we will gaze on the infinite glory of the infinite God. The joy of heaven will be the contemplation of this glorious God.

When we finally arrive in the place described in the last pages of the Bible, we will come to understand the purpose and value of every sorrow that has ever touched our lives. We will agree with the apostle Paul:

> I consider that our present sufferings are not worth comparing
> with the glory that will be revealed in us. For the creation waits
> in eager expectation for the children of God to be revealed.
> For the creation was subjected to frustration, not by its own
> choice, but by the will of the one who subjected it, in hope that
> the creation itself will be liberated from its bondage to decay
> and brought into the freedom and glory of the children of God.
> (Romans 8:18–21)

And again:

> Therefore we do not lose heart. Though outwardly we are
> wasting away, yet inwardly we are being renewed day by day. For
> our light and momentary troubles are achieving for us an eternal
> glory that far outweighs them all. So we fix our eyes not on what
> is seen, but on what is unseen, since what is seen is temporary,
> but what is unseen is eternal.
> (2 Corinthians 4:16–18)

Surely, the best is yet to be.

Notes

1. The power and prevalence of pain

1. The hymn is 'Come, See If There Ever Was Sorrow Like His' by Charles Wesley.
2. Elisabeth Elliot's website: www.elisabethelliot.org, March 2003.

2. Clearing the decks of false ideas

1. 'Thought for the Day', *The Today Programme*, BBC Radio 4.
2. From Martin Luther's *Table Talk*.

3. A word from another world

1. *Mail Online*, 7 January 2009 (http://www.dailymail.co.uk/sciencetech/article-1106884/Three-second-memory-myth-Fish-remember-months.html).
2. Nicholos Wethington, Universe Today (www.universetoday.com), December 2008.
3. This quote has also been variously attributed to John Bunyan, D. L. Moody and C. S. Lewis!
4. Deuteronomy 8:2–3; Matthew 4:4.

4. Living in a broken world

1. The hymn is 'Our God, Our Help in Ages Past' by Isaac Watts.
2. Woody Allen, 2004.

3. The hymn is 'O Worship the King, All Glorious Above' by Robert Grant.

4. 'Before the Throne of God Above' by Charitie Lees Bancroft and Vikki Cook.

5. Jim Elliot, quoted in Elisabeth Elliot, *Shadow of the Almighty* (HarperCollins, 1989), p. 149.

5. Knowing the One who knows us perfectly

1. Cambridge University Library website: www.lib.cam.ac.uk

2. *The Hiding Place* (Chosen Books, 1971), written by Corrie ten Boom together with John and Elizabeth Sherrill.

3. 'Ask the Van', University of Illinois, Department of Physics website: http://van.physics.illinois.edu/qa

4. David Watson, *Fear No Evil* (Hodder Christian Paperbacks, 1984).

6. Perfect way, perfect purposes

1. Whitefield quote, cited in John Piper, *The Hidden Smile of God* (Crossway, 2001), p. 61.

2. John Bunyan, *Grace Abounding to the Chief of Sinners* (Evangelical Press, 1978), p. 123.

3. Ibid., p. 121.

8. Reasons to be cheerful

1. John Owen, *Communion with God* (Banner of Truth, 1991), cited in Jerry Bridges, *The Discipline of Grace* (NavPress, 2006), p. 127.

9. Living with uncertainty

1. Nursing Assistant Central, '100 Fascinating Facts You Never Knew about the Human Brain': www.nursingassistantcentral.com/blog/2008/100-fascinating-facts-you-never-knew-about-the-human-brain

2. Ibid.

3. www.simonguillebaud.com/blog/1-general/98-revival-praying-and-chalk-circles

4. For more about Hudson Taylor, see Roger Steer, *J. Hudson Taylor: A Man in Christ* (Authentic Media, 2005).

5. Random Facts, 'Facts about the human heart': http://facts.randomhistory.com/human-heart-facts.html

10. Don't waste your sorrows

1. For more about Hudson Taylor, see Roger Steer, *J. Hudson Taylor: A Man in Christ* (Authentic Media, 2005).

2. Wholesome Words: www.wholesomewords.org. *Missionary Biographies – John G. Paton: The Apostle of Christ to the Cannibals* by Eugene Myers Harrison.

3. Charles H. Spurgeon, sermon on 2 Corinthians 12:9, *The Metropolitan Tabernacle Pulpit* (Banner of Truth, 1992).

11. The love that will not let us go

1. Actually, this is a common misconception. MS sufferers will tell you that there can be severe bouts of pain.

2. 'Before the Throne of God Above' by Charitie Lees Bancroft and Vikki Cook.

3. From Martin Luther's *Table Talk*.

4. The hymn is 'How Firm a Foundation' by Richard Keene.

5. The hymn is 'O Love That Will Not Let Me Go' by George Matteson.

12. Living in hope

1. www.biblestudytools.com/commentaries/revelation/revelation-21/revelation-21-16.html

2. Lifestyle Lounge, 'Facts about the Atlantic Ocean': http://lifestyle.iloveindia.com/lounge/facts-about-atlantic-ocean-3522.html

related titles from IVP

Remember
The things that matter when hope is hard to find
Rhonda Watson

ISBN: 978-1-84474-545-6
192 pages, paperback

Rhonda Watson models how to remember God during times of physical suffering. Packed full of poetry, songs and Bible quotes, this beautiful devotional guide helps readers face failing physical powers with honesty, and focus on the character of God, the source of our hope. 'My soul is downcast within me; therefore I will remember you.'

Diagnosed in 2008 with Motor Neurone Disease (MND), Rhonda Watson was rapidly losing her speech, mobility and other physical functions. In desperation she turned to the only true source of hope and comfort – God.

This honest and powerful book helps fellow-sufferers recall in times of trouble the character of God – who walks with us along the path of suffering and holds us in our pain. Choosing not to focus on her own debilitating condition, Rhonda provides devotions and reflections which have helped her, and will encourage the reader to hold on to trust in Jesus.

With space for journaling, this book is ideal for anyone coping with disability and failing physical powers.

'As a chronically ill, disabled person, I found this book authentic, helpful, encouraging and challenging. I warmly recommend it to anyone who is suffering.' Dr Emily Ackerman

Available from your local Christian bookshop or **www.thinkivp.com**

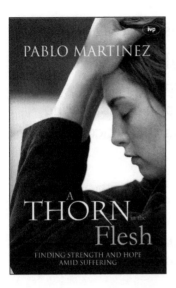

Sharon Dirckx
Foreword by Ravi Zacharias

why?

Looking at God, evil
& personal suffering

related titles from IVP

Why?
Looking at God, evil & personal suffering
Sharon Dirckx

ISBN: 978-1-84474-619-4
176 pages, paperback

Suffering and tragedy can cause us all to ask 'Why?' Why do bad things happen? If God exists, does he care? Of all the hurdles to faith, surely suffering must be the greatest. It tears lives apart and raises questions for us all. But when we ask 'Why?', to whom are we addressing our question? Where do the most satisfying answers come from? Does it matter?

Sharon Dirckx unpacks our questions sensitively and wisely, weaving her arguments with real-life stories of anguish and pain. She concludes, 'I would like to show you that, even though we don't understand everything, it is still possible to believe in a powerful, loving God and acknowledge the reality of evil and suffering. Not only that, but seeing life from this perspective helps us make more, not less, sense of our hurting world.' While we may never have all the answers, it does not mean that there are no answers at all.

'This book is not just about suffering, but written by one who knows suffering to others who are suffering themselves.'
Os Guinness

Available from your local Christian bookshop or **www.thinkivp.com**

For more information about IVP
and our publications visit
www.ivpbooks.com

Get regular updates at **ivpbooks.com/signup**
Find us on **facebook.com/ivpbooks**
Follow us on **twitter.com/ivpbookcentre**

Inter-Varsity Press, a company limited by guarantee registered in England and Wales, number 05202650. Registered office IVP Bookcentre, Norton Street, Nottingham NG7 3HR, United Kingdom. Registered charity number 1105757.